Power in Tudor England

British Studies Series

General Editor: JEREMY BLACK

Published

Forthcoming

Power in Tudor England

David Loades
Professor of History
University of Wales, Bangor

First published 1997 by
MACMILLAN PRESS LTD
Houndmills, Basingstoke, Hampshire RG21 6XS
and London
Companies and representatives
throughout the world

ISBN 0–333–59836–9 hardcover
ISBN 0–333–59837–7 paperback

A catalogue record for this book is available
from the British Library.

10   9   8   7   6   5   4   3   2   1
06   05   04   03   02   01   00   99   98   97

Copy-edited and typeset by Povey–Edmondson
Okehampton and Rochdale, England

Printed in Hong Kong

 Published in the United States of America 1997 by
ST.MARTIN'S PRESS, INC.,
Scholarly and Reference Division
175 Fifth Avenue, New York, N.Y. 10010

ISBN 0–312–16391–6 (cloth)
ISBN 0–312–16392–4 (pbk.)

Contents

List of Maps

Glossary

advowson The right to present to an ecclesiastical living or benefice.

apange Literally 'privilege'; used of substantial jurisdictional franchises or peculiars, normally accompanying grants of large estates.

bouge of court The right to be fed at the king's table; a privilege of those who held Chamber or Household office.

certiorari A writ, issued out of Chancery or King's Bench, enabling proceedings made by any court of record, or by provincial officials, to be removed and certified before the superior courts at Westminster.

first fruits and tenths Dues from bishoprics and other major ecclesiastical preferments, originally paid to the pope, but transferred to the Crown by a statute of 1534. First fruits were in theory a full year's revenue of the benefice. Tenths were a regular annual tax, in theory 10 per cent of the value.

General Eyre Visitation by the royal justices, similar to the later assizes. Henry II divided England into six circuits, and sent out itinerant justices in groups of three. They were empowered to hear all pleas of the Crown.

nisi prius A writ so called because it ordered the sheriff to cause jurors, summoned to be present at actions put down for trial in the central courts, to appear at Westminster before a specified day 'unless before' the circuit judges should visit his county.

mignon A favourite; used specifically of the king's favourites, especially the 'gentilshommes de la chambre'.

oyer and terminer A judicial commission issued by the Crown to a group of named individuals, conferring upon them the power to 'hear and determine' certain cases. Such commissions might be limited by time, or area, or confined to a single case.

Provisors and Praemunire A group of statutes passed between 1363 and 1393, restricting papal rights to appoint to benefices in England, and prohibiting the exercise of ecclesiastical jurisdiction without the king's consent.

socage   A traditional tenure by non-military service.
supersedeas   A writ issued to cancel or annul any normal
    judicial process.
terminari   A writ used to move an indictment into the central
    courts when a defendant wished to plead error of process.

Preamble: A Personal Monarchy

Late medieval England was the most centralised and unified monarchy in Europe. This was partly the result of accident, and partly of design. It had been the accident of conquest in 1066 which had enabled William I to create a feudal structure in England which had largely avoided the problems of seigneurial jurisdictions. Similarly it was accident, or at least impersonal circumstances, which dictated that there should be only one great urban centre. On the other hand it was the design of Henry II and his successors which created the great unifying force of common law, and which harnessed it to the king's purposes. The basic jurisdictional units of shire and hundred were already old when William secured the throne, and that enabled him to avoid basing his government upon the tenants-in-chief. At the same time, since England was relatively small and free from impassable wildernesses, internal communications were easy, and swift by comparison with France or the Holy Roman Empire. For all these and other reasons, Edward III and Henry V had been able to mobilise their comparatively modest resources with a speed and completeness which had made them more than a match for the much larger and more populous kingdom of France, and to hold large parts of that country in subjection for generations. As early as the twelfth century, several of the major institutions of government had gone 'out of court'. The Exchequer, the Chancery, and the principal common law courts of King's Bench and Common Pleas became permanently located at Westminster, within a stone's throw of the great city of London. The Church had apparently defeated attempts at enhanced royal control in the reigns of Henry II and John, but in the last decade of the fourteenth century, while the papacy had been weakened by the Great Schism, the English parliament had enacted the statutes of Provisors and Praemunire.[1] Although it would be an exaggeration to say that these Acts prefigured the royal supremacy, they did indicate that the king of England regarded the *Ecclesia Anglicana* as his own territory, upon which no one intruded without permission. Moreover, by the late fifteenth century the chances of inheritance had enhanced the process of unification still further. The Duchy of Lancaster, the Duchy of Cornwall, the Earldom of Chester and the Earldom of March had all fallen to the Crown. These great secular franchises had been established in the early Middle Ages, in contrast to normal royal policy, to facilitate the control of remote and lawless parts of the kingdom. Had they continued in the hands of great noble families, neither the Yorkists nor the Tudors would have been able to govern as they did, but the last of them came into the king's hands in 1461, leaving only the ecclesiastical franchise of Durham outside direct control. The fact that the king's writ ran in the name of the Duke of Cornwall or the Earl of Chester affected the form rather than the substance of royal control. The princi- pality of Wales was similar, except that it had always been intended as an acceptable front for direct rule. Sometimes there was a Prince of Wales, and sometimes there was not,[2] but in either case the principality was governed by officials appointed by the king. Except for the bishopric of Durham, where the bishop was virtually a royal servant, and a few minor lordships in the marches of Wales, the king's writ ran, under one guise or another, throughout his realm. No other monarch in Europe could boast as much.

However, anyone witnessing the lively aristocratic feuding of the 1450s, and the creeping paralysis which had afflicted the govern- ment of Henry VI, could have been forgiven for not noticing this constitutional strength. When nobles or powerful gentry could capture or intimidate the institutions through which the king ruled, the situation actually became worse than if they had possessed their own proper jurisdiction, because an element of irresponsibility was added to their power. By 1455 it looked as though the discontinu- ance of the General Eyre, which had concentrated the attention of the royal justices on specific areas for long periods, had been a gesture of overconfidence. The General Eyre had disappeared by the end of the thirteenth century, and although its effectiveness had been limited, it had not been adequately replaced. The justices of assize were helpless in the face of powerful and recalcitrant retinues, while the offices of sheriff and justice of the peace were vigorously exploited for individual or partisan ends. As John Heydon ob- served, he would sooner forfeit £1,000 than lose the office of Sheriff of Norfolk, so profitable had he been able to make it.[3] However, what the king's weakness had relinquished the king's strength could redeem. Before his death in 1483 Edward IV had recovered all the ground which had been lost by his predecessor. Faced in 1461 with a system of government which appeared to be in total collapse, he had improvised his tactics along traditional lines. Uncertain for some time where he could repose his trust, he relied heavily on his household and on a select band of nobles and ecclesiastics. This was entirely justifiable, because otherwise it would have been impossible to stop the Yorkist affinity in the counties from behaving like a victorious faction and perpetuating the feuds which he urgently needed to reconcile and end. It would not have helped the cause of justice, for example, to have replaced Sir John Heydon with Sir John Paston as Sheriff of Norfolk and in November 1461 Edward sent down a trusted household knight, Sir Thomas Montgomery, 'to set a rule in the county'. Nevertheless the rise of household government, which included using the Treasury of the Chamber as the king's main revenue department, had some serious drawbacks. Most particularly, it depended far too heavily upon the monarch's personal involvement and control.

Edward delegated great powers to his brother, the Duke of Gloucester, to his brother-in-law Earl Rivers, and to his Chamberlain, Lord Hastings. A small number of other peers were similarly favoured, notably the Duke of Buckingham and the Earl of Northumberland. They were all men of great power in their 'countries', and therein lay their usefulness to the king, but in spite of their personal loyalty to him, he never succeeded in welding them into a team.[4] He probably never tried, because the concept would have been alien to him, but as a result his government fell apart on his death, and within five years the Yorkist affinity had destroyed itself. The danger with household government was that, like the spoils system in nineteenth-century America, it made continuity from one reign to the next very difficult. It also emphasised personal loyalty to the king at the expense of impersonal loyalty to the Crown, a distinction which fifteenth-century lawyers and royal servants were perfectly capable of making. Consequently the success of the Tudors after 1485 arose from the fact that Henry VII perceived the complexity of the challenge which confronted him. It was not only necessary to restore the authority of a Crown shaken for the second time in a generation by usurpation and brief civil war; it was also necessary to restore it in such a way that it rested upon the underlying strength of the institution rather than the personalities of the incumbent and his immediate servants. Henry, with his background of exile and poverty, and his miscellaneous assortment of supporters, was in some ways ideally placed to do that. Necessity drove him in the direction which acute political intelligence might have suggested. Pathologically insecure for most of his reign, he did not even trust his uncle, the Duke of Bedford, as Edward had trusted Richard of Gloucester. Because of this his style of government became distributive. 'Study to serve me, and I will study to enrich you', he is alleged to have said to Sir Henry Wyatt. Many men of all ranks, including nobles, were trusted up to a point, and moderately rewarded when that trust was justified. It was in some ways parsimonious method, and it was not very popular, but it worked. Moreover it set precedents which his son and grand-children were to follow for almost a century after his death – a century which was to transform the political structure of England.

In order to understand the realities of power in the sixteenth century, it is not sufficient to grasp the constitutional structure. The importance of great private households, so conspicuous in the fifteenth century, steadily ebbed away under the pressures of royal policy. In their place appeared a much broader ruling class, the 'political nation', linked to the Crown directly by a network of offices and preferments. It was this network, and the way in which it was used which created the 'increase of governance', noted by contemporaries, and examined by generations of historians. By the end of Elizabeth's reign England was highly unified, but not particularly centralised. The queen's writ ran uniformly from Ramsgate to Holyhead, and from Bodmin to Berwick, but the professional bureaucracy numbered only a fraction of that of France or Castile. Elizabeth knew perfectly well that her power was restricted, although she would never have admitted the fact. It was restricted by those same men who upheld it, and the limitation was the price of their support. The queen could not tax at will, and she could not make law without the consent of parliament. Nor could she enforce law without the cooperation of her more sub-stantial subjects. Just as a feudal monarchy had rested upon the contract of homage between the king and his tenants-in-chief, Tudor monarchy rested upon an unwritten understanding between the monarch and the 'political nation'. It was a relationship of mutual advantage. In return for their services in office, men received not salaries, or even fees necessarily, but prestige, patron-age and opportunities for profit. In Elizabethan Norfolk gentlemen intrigued and competed fiercely, not merely to secure a place upon the commission of the peace, but to secure a higher place the next time the commission was issued.[5] Yet the duties of a justice of the peace could be onerous, and the tangible rewards uncertain.

The English nobility had never monopolised the 'political nation', although they had controlled it briefly during the troubles of the fifteenth century. During the sixteenth century they continued to form an important part of it, but gradually lost power to the gentry, less wealthy individually, but far more numerous. Moreover the 'political nation' extended beyond the aristocracy to include those numerous local officers of yeoman rank whose services were almost as crucial to social stability as those of their betters. Parish constables and church wardens might be looked down upon, and even mocked by courtly wits, but if they had ever become seriously disaffected law enforcement would have broken down at the point of contact. The towns had by long tradition their own governing elites, who were equally part of the 'political nation', but in England, unlike some parts of Europe, they were not particularly powerful. Only London could command serious political attention, although second-rank cities such as Norwich or York were not without weight in issues which directly concerned them. The 'political nation' was not articulated in any sophisticated theory but depended partly upon pragmatism and partly upon the ancient and respectable principle of consent. The common law was in one sense the king's law, but more importantly it was the law of the whole community, evolved over many centuries to meet a collective need. It was therefore 'owned' by everyone with a stake in the realm, even a small one. Up to a point the monarchy was seen in the same way – it was ordained by God to protect and lead the community of the realm. Obedience was therefore not only a duty to God but an action of self-interest, and participation in the processes of government a natural and expected responsibility. This was not democracy in the modern sense, because it was proportionately linked to wealth and status, but it did lead to a far more broadly based government than most continental observers were used to. 'Ce royaulme est populaire' ('this kingdom is controlled by the people'), wrote Simon Reynard to Charles V in 1553 when he was endeavouring to explain how the apparently invincible force deployed by the Duke of Northumberland had simply melted away during the succession crisis of July. In so far as this diffuse sense of ownership was articulated into an institution, it was the parliament, and particularly the House of Commons.

> For every Englishman is intended to be there present either in person or by procuration and attorneys, of what preeminence, state, dignity or quality soever he be, from the prince (be he king or queen) to the lowest person in England. And the consent of the parliament is taken to be every man's consent.[6]

When the gentlemen of middle England decided that the king was a better lord than the Earl of Derby or the Duke of Buckingham, they were creating a new system of priorities, the implications of which extended far beyond personal loyalties.

Parliament was one of the three 'points of contact' between the Tudors and their subjects, identified by Geoffrey Elton in his presidential addresses to the Royal Historical Society twenty years ago.[7] The others were the court and the Council. The court had always been a principal theatre of monarchy – the place where the king displayed his magnificence, and to which he attracted service. Like their predecessors, the Tudors employed a hard core of professional courtiers and servants, but they spread the net of part-time service far more widely. Gentlemen ushers and other Chamber servants worked three-month shifts, quadrupling the number of those who could claim court office without greatly increasing the cost. Virtually every county in England, and many in Wales, were represented among the king's gentlemen at the end of Henry's reign, spreading the tentacles of the royal affinity widely among the local elites. By contrast the Council had long since lost any representative function which it might once have possessed. Even the diffuse Council of Henry VII consisted of royal advisers and officials, whilst the more tightly organised Privy Council from 1535 onwards was a working executive with a heavy burden of routine. On the other hand it was the Council to which local officers of all kinds were ultimately responsible. Receivers were responsible in the first instance to the appropriate revenue department, and sheriffs accounted to the Exchequer but if any complaint of abuse or malfeasance were upheld against them, it was to the Council that they were summoned. The Council sent out regular letters of instruction and admonition to the commissions of the peace, and guided the justices' work, particularly in matters of police and administration. After 1535 the Council also busied itself constantly with the royal ecclesiastical jurisdiction. Clergy were summoned to answer for unsatisfactory sermons, and bishops were occasionally imprisoned for recalcitrance. The Council, usually guided and serviced by the royal secretaries, was the workhorse of central government. Its network of informants and the close personal contacts between its members and the county elites kept it in constant touch with local politics, both secular and ecclesiastical.

All of these institutions were important for the give and take of effective government, but the real secret of Tudor success lay in the use of the royal commissions. A commission was a legal instrument whereby the monarch conferred upon a group of named individuals the authority to perform certain specified tasks on his behalf. Some commissions were *ad hoc*, such as those for the conduct of musters or collection of a subsidy; others, notably the commission of the peace, were standing. Some authorised the conduct of an investigation, others the exercise of judicial power; others again were purely administrative. The commission was a highly flexible instrument, and it worked because all parties stood to gain. The king recruited the cooperation and knowledge of local community leaders, harnessing their authority to his purposes. The nobility, gentry and lawyers who served gained a visible and honourable display of royal confidence, which enhanced their prestige and gave them access to superior opportunities of patronage. Nor was it always clear to their inferiors and dependants when they were speaking in the king's name, and when in their own. This was an immense advantage when it came, for example, to fixing wage rates in the Elizabethan period. The commission was the essential 'transmission system' which communicated the directing will of the monarch into the power structures of counties, towns and villages.

> There never was in any common wealth devised a more wise, a more dulce and gentle, nor more certain way to rule the people, whereby they are kept always as it were in a bridle of good order, and sooner looked unto that they should not offend than punished when they have offended.[8]

Smith was not free from the weakness of complacency, but without the system of commissions, the underfunded government of Tudor

England could not have worked at all. Unable to tax at will, the Tudors could never have afforded a network of paid officials. The normal European alternative, dependence upon noble affinities, had created more problems than it had solved in the fifteenth century and the Tudors were forced to improvise. The result struck such a good balance between central control and local autonomy that it endured for more than four hundred years.

The most comprehensive study of this subtle blend of unity and diversity is Penry William's *The Tudor Regime*, first published in 1979. Since then a number of local studies have appeared, of which the best is probably Diarmaid MacCulloch's *Suffolk and the Tudors* (1986). There have been good studies of individual noblemen, such as Stephen Gunn's *Charles Brandon, Duke of Suffolk*, and of the nobility collectively, notably Helen Miller's *Henry VIII and the English Nobility* (1986), and George Bernard's *The Tudor Nobility* (1992). However, there has been, as far as I am aware, no attempt within a brief compass to examine the whole structure of the body politic, in terms of its bones and sinews. What follows is not a constitutional history, nor a social history. I am not much interested in the evolution of statute law, nor in the creation of wealth, much less the role of women or the rise of Protestant theology. My concern is to analyse, in as succinct and comprehensible a manner as possible, the interaction between the central machinery of government – Crown, Council, court, Chancery, Exchequer, Common Benches and parliament – and the local and provincial elites who, by virtue of their wealth or ancestry 'bore rule' within their own communities. In the aftermath of the Pilgrimage of Grace Henry VIII had declared: 'we will not be bound of a necessity to be served with Lords. But we will be served with such men of what degree soever as we shall appoint to the same'.[9] It was a somewhat premature boast as far as the north of England was concerned, but Elizabeth achieved it after 1569. Neither Henry nor Elizabeth was aiming to install the equivalent of a French intendant, and the gentlemen who eventually ruled the north in their monarch's name, like those who ruled most of England, were the grandsons and greatgrandsons of those who had served in the affinities of Percy or Mowbray or Stafford.

Sixteenth-century England was a personal monarchy, but it was no longer the monarch's private lordship. In one sense the Tudors were perceived, and perceived themselves, as agents of God. They did not own England, and they acknowledged responsibilities towards their subjects. At the same time they were more than chief executives. Unlike an elected president, a monarch could not legitimately be removed for misgovernment. The only ground upon which a subject's allegiance could be annulled was that the *de facto* ruler was not, in fact, the lawful king or queen. Because the monarchy was personal, the characters and abilities of the incumbents were of critical importance, as were their illnesses, marriages, fertility and death. The monarch was the keystone in the arch of government: the shaper of policy and the maker of decisions. What follows is not a history of the Tudor monarchy, but an analysis of power structures to which the monarchy is at all times central and essential. Even in Tudor England not all authority was exercised in the king's name, but it is appropriate that the period from 1485 to 1603 should be identified in English history by the name of the ruling dynasty.

Notes

1. There were four such Acts against papal provisions between 1351 and 1389, and three statutes of praemunire in 1353, 1365 and 1393. The last was the so-called 'Great Statute', which was a protest against threats by Pope Boniface IX to excommunicate English bishops who obeyed the decisions of the king's courts concerning advowsons. It was the 'Great Statute' which was used by Henry VIII against the clergy in 1532.

2. There was a Prince of Wales almost continuously from 1284 to 1413; and then from 1454 to 1484, from 1489 to 1502, and from 1504 to 1509. The title was not used again during the Tudor period. See J. G. Edwards, *The Principality of Wales, 1267–1969* (1969); J. Davies, *Hanes Cymru [History of Wales]* (1990).

3. James Gresham to John Paston, *Paston Letters*, vol. I, ed. J. Gairdner (1910) p. 157.

4. C. Ross, *Edward IV* (1974) pp. 331–41.

5. A. Hassell Smith, *Country and Court: Government and Politics in Norfolk, 1558–1603* (1974) pp. 51–86.

6. Sir Thomas Smith, *De Republica Anglorum*, ed. M. Dewar (1982) pp. 78–9.

7. G. R. Elton, *Studies in Tudor and Stuart Politics and Government*, vol. III (1983) pp. 3–21, reprinted from *Transactions of the Royal Historical Society* 24 (1974).

8. Smith, *De Republica Anglorum*, p. 106.

9. D. Loades, *Politics and the Nation, 1450–1660* (1992) p. 203.

1 The Nature of Authority

All authority derived ultimately from God. As Thomas Cranmer's *Homily on Obedience*, once of those pieces authorised to be read in churches in the absence of a sermon, put it in 1547:

> Almighty God hath created and appointed all things in heaven, earth and waters in most excellent and perfect order. In heaven he hath appointed distinct orders and states of archangels and angels. In the earth he has assigned kings, princes, with other governors under them, all in good and necessary order.[1]

Consequently obedience to established authority was a religious duty, but the order envisaged by the homilist was less perfect than he imagined. God worked perforce through human agents, and these were not necessarily arranged in neat hierarchies. There had for centuries been disputes between spiritual and temporal lords over priorities, and the demarcation between their respective jurisdictions. Although the Church had never publicly admitted it, by the end of the fifteenth century this long-drawn-out struggle had ended in compromise. Kings accepted the papal primacy in theory, but largely ignored it in practice. Popes acquiesced in this situation in order to retain the support and cooperation of the secular authorities in the preservation of ecclesiastical discipline. There was no universally accepted theory of the relationship between kings and popes, which tended to be settled by *ad hoc* concordats such as that between Francis I and Leo X in 1516. It was partly for that reason that Clement VII had not at first taken Henry VIII's threats of schism seriously. Nor did Henry or his subjects understand at first the full implications of what he had done. From 1534 onward, with the exception of the years 1554–8, it was treason to assert the papal primacy in England, but that enhanced rather than diminished the divine credentials of the English monarchy. To challenge the royal supremacy was to challenge the will of God as that became understood by the consensus of English opinion.

It might have been expected, therefore, that England would have been in the vanguard of those countries embracing the Divine

Right of Kings. However, that was not the case. English kings had toyed with absolutist pretensions in the past, and had been brutally disciplined by their recalcitrant subjects. John had survived at the price of surrender, and Richard II had not survived at all. In both cases the aristocracy had insisted upon the contractual nature of their feudal allegiance, but the principle which they invoked was corporate rather than personal. In practice it was the noble retinues which kept the king within bounds, but in theory it was the law. 'Debet rex esse sub lege' ('the king should rule under the law') had written the authoritative thirteenth-century commentator Henry de Bracton, and in so far as there was a recognised legislative body for the common law, it was the whole body of the realm. It was a basic precept of all medieval jurisprudence that positive law must be consistent with, and subordinate to, the laws of God and Nature. Great quantities of ink had been consumed in the learned definition of these concepts, but what they amounted to in practice was a code of conduct derived from the Bible, particularly the New Testament, reinforced with certain aspects of Greek philosophy derived mainly from Aristotle. That the common law did not transgress the boundaries thus identified was not a question of restraining a sovereign will, but of developing a judicial consensus. In that sense the law was the voice of both God and the people. 'Vox populi vox dei' ('the voice of the people is the voice of God') was a precept quoted by medieval jurists only when it suited them but the fact that it was a familiar tag should remind us that there was more than one theory about the transmission of divine authority. Kings might have been the Lord's Anointed, but it was not only the Church which denied them a monopoly of God's favour. England, wrote Sir John Fortescue in the late fifteenth century, was a *dominium politicum et regale*, that is to say a realm in which the royal authority was both supported and restrained by constitutional means, and of these the chief was the common law.[2]

To this balance the king's ecclesiastical supremacy posed an obvious threat. Common lawyers writing in the 1530s, such as Christopher St German, were insistent that Henry's newly recognised authority could no more override the temporal law than that of the pope which it replaced. Fortunately, whatever the theoretical framework, the king could not, by his own act, create new offences which touched the lives or property of his subjects. Treasons and felonies could only be created by Act of Parliament, and if Henry wished to enforce his new jurisdiction, it could only be by that means. Consequently parliament became a partner in the ecclesiastical revolution, a development which also had the immense advantage of enabling the king to appeal to the 'consent of the realm' for support in all that he did. Nobody at the time, least of all Henry himself, thought of the royal supremacy as being either created or exercised through parliament – but then no one thought of the common law as having been created by parliament either. It is only with hindsight that we see the Act of Restraint of Appeals or the Act of Supremacy as marking the emergence of a sovereign legislative will in England. However there were immediate practical consequences. The king began to tax the Church, not merely through clerical subsidies, which he had received before, but through first-fruits and tenths. He began to tamper with the calendar, and to demolish the great pilgrimage shrines. Soon after he dissolved the monasteries and appropriated their vast estates. All this was done with the consent of the 'political nation', as expressed by parliament. Within a few years of Henry's death the worship and doctrine of the English Church were converted to Protestantism by the same means, and then converted back again.

By the time that Elizabeth came to the throne in 1558 no one doubted that the proper, and indeed the only, way to construct a religious settlement was through parliament. At the same time, although judicial interpretation continued to be used, by the time that Sir Thomas Smith was writing in 1565, the only way to make any significant amendments or extensions to the common law was by statute.

Fortescue's maxims were not challenged in principle until the reign of James I. The Tudors carefully avoided any definition of exactly how the common law restrained the monarch. Even Henry VIII, who executed two wives and a number of senior royal servants because they had temporarily displeased him, was always careful to use the due process of law.[3] Nor did the Tudors dismiss judges for political reasons. When they wished to transgress the existing law, they got parliament to alter it for them first. Nevertheless sixteenth-century lawyers did not really trust the judiciary to defend the law against abuse or subversion by the Crown. Hence their enthusiasm for parliament, and the large number of them who obtained seats in the House of Commons by the reign of Elizabeth. By the early seventeenth century the preservation of the *dominium politicum* had come to depend very largely upon the Lords and Commons assembled at Westminster which is why the frequency of sessions had become such an important issue by the reign of Charles I.

Parliament did not enact canon law, but neither did anyone else. The law of the church had been created and developed by General Councils and by the papacy. In England local canons had been enacted by the convocations of the provinces of York and Canterbury. Henry VIII forbade the study of canon law in the universities, but he did not forbid its practice, and those parts of the traditional code which did not refer to, or depend upon the papacy, continued in force. Sporadic attempts were made between 1535 and 1553 to produce a new code appropriate to the English Church, but these were finally abandoned when Edward VI's Council decided that a code enacted by parliament might have too much authority, and codes produced by the convocations would raise too many questions about the autonomy of the Church. It was not to be until 1604 that new canons were approved, and until then the ecclesiastical courts continued to operate with the remains of the old code. Since appeal from these courts ultimately lay to the monarch as Supreme Head or Supreme Governor, they were in a sense royal courts, but they were not conducted in the king's name, except for a few years under Edward VI.[4] If the canon law had ever been a serious competitor with the common law, that situation was ended by the Submission of the Clergy in 1532. Because of its restricted competence it could never in any case have challenged most of the common law's functions. The real secular rival should have been the civil or Roman law, derived from the ancient codes of the Emperor Justinian. Roman law was being received in many parts of Europe at this time, including Scotland. It was rightly regarded as being more sympathetic to royal authority than most of the customary codes, bearing maxims such as 'quod principi placuit, legis habet vigorem' ('that which pleases the prince has the force of law') – which was almost the antithesis of Bracton. However, the strength of the common law, and the fact that it already extended to the whole of England, deterred the Tudors from making any serious attempt to raise the civil law. It was used only in the Admiralty Courts, under the guise of *Lex Maritima*, which was the nearest thing then existing to the international law of later generations.

The only secular courts which were not conducted in the king's name after the legislation of 1536 were those of honours and manors, where the law administered was that of local custom. 'Custom of the manor' did not extend to any criminal offences, all of which were pleas of the Crown, but dealt with such day-to-day matters as damage inflicted by straying animals, disputes over field boundaries, and above all the tenancies of the manor and their transmission. Customary law could not contradict or override the common law, of which it had originally been part, but no appeal could lie from a manor court to a common law court such as the quarter sessions or the assizes. Appeal was possible to the equity side of Chancery, which emphasised that even manorial courts were ultimately subject to the king's authority, but the king's law officers did not interfere in the internal affairs of honours or manors. Unlike the law in any of its various forms, equity belonged exclusively to the king. The Lord Chancellor, who had the principal responsibility for administering it, was significantly called 'the keeper of the king's conscience'. Equity was designed to provide justice in those cases which the law did not cover, or for which the common law courts were in some way inadequate. As Lord Chancellor, Cardinal Wolsey created the equity courts of Star Chamber and Requests, using the all-purpose authority of the king's Council. By the early seventeenth century the common lawyers had become very suspicious of the 'conciliar courts', seeing them as their predecessors had seen the royal supremacy – another possible means by which the *dominium politicum* might be subverted. As long as Elizabeth was alive this fear remained subdued, not least because she had no time for theories of Divine Right monarchy. This was partly because she was a pragmatist, who realised only too clearly how far her power rested upon the consent and cooperation of her subjects, and partly because Divine Right implied a theory of the transmission of power, as well as of its exercise. Just as a Divine Right monarch was answerable only to God for his or her actions, so only God, by the genetic process of heredity, could determine the transmission of the title. This was much more specific than the general notion that royal authority derived from God. Indefeasible hereditary right did not recognise constitutional law, and Elizabeth's title to the throne rested upon her father's last succession Act of 1543.[5] When Mary Tudor died in November 1558, the only heir of undoubted legitimacy was Mary Stuart, the granddaughter of Henry VIII's elder sister Margaret. Mary had virtually no support in England at that time. She had been ignored in Henry's succession Act, and was regarded as a foreigner, but she remained in the wings and forced Elizabeth, probably against her own inclinations, to take a constitutional view of the succession. James's position, however, owed nothing to positive law and everything to the hereditary principle, so it is not surprising that he displayed a quite different attitude to the Divine Right of Kings, conveniently ignoring the other half of the equation.

In 1600 God still spoke to the English in a variety of ways. Only two of them mattered politically, the voice of the monarch, and the voice of the *populus*, or political nation, which was heard in different ways in the common law and in parliament, but other voices had not entirely disappeared. A sheriff or a justice of the peace spoke for the king, and his authority was exercised by delegation. But a nobleman or a substantial gentleman exercised power in his 'country' which was autonomous, or 'natural'. This was not created simply by wealth or royal favour. The Earl of Bedford held vast estates in the south-west of England, but as Lord John Russell he had been quite unable to control the popular discontent in Devon and Cornwall in 1549 until he had a mercenary army at his back. In 1553 the Duke of Northumberland was the richest and most powerful subject of the Crown, but he had no 'country' to fall back on when his control of the Council disintegrated. On the other hand a family like the Tyrells, who were never of more than minor importance in national affairs, had lived in the same corner of Essex for generations, and were readily followed and obeyed by their neighbours and dependants. Such a position, which derived partly from wealth, but more from lineage and inherited qualities of leadership, was regarded as God-given. It was also a position carrying responsibility. Such a man was expected to provide generous hospitality for his neighbours, to give alms to the poor, to support his parish church, showing suitable piety on the traditional occasions, and to be just in administering the custom of his manors. In other words his respect or 'manred' was part of a mutual relationship with the community in which he lived. None of this owed anything to the king, and very little to the law. It was a lifestyle much respected by those traditional moralists known as the 'commonwealth men', but by the mid-century it was under serious threat. Various factors had contributed to that situation. The decline of the great affinities under pressure from the Crown had to some extent disorientated local loyalties, creating direct links to the king which compromised many such families when Henry VIII began to pursue controversial and unpopular policies. More importantly, the dissolution of the monasteries and the opportunities which that created disrupted relationships which had existed for generations and set family against family. The religious changes which were already apparent by 1547 had an even more disruptive effect, dividing kindreds and setting sons against fathers. Eventually this was to prove a very creative disruption, but at the time many saw it as evidence of divine wrath. Preachers and moralists denounced those gentlemen who took their opportunities as:

Men without conscience. Men utterly void of God's fear. Yea, men that live as though there were no God at all.[6]

Not surprisingly, such statements fanned the flames of popular discontent, and something remarkably like class hatred appeared in the turbulent summers of 1548 and 1549. The natural order seemed to be dissolving as countrymen rose against their lords, and gentlemen found their servants deserting them to join the malcontents. Of course it was not the end of the world. Within a year order had been restored, and no such general crisis was to occur again. Nevertheless, there was a subtle change in the nature of rural life. The decline of traditional values was accelerated and by the end of the century old-fashioned housekeeping was lamented as a lost art. More importantly, the authority of the gentleman in his 'country' was never quite the same again; more now rested upon the king, and less on lordship.

A further consequence of the decline in private affinities was the increasingly specific use of the term 'servant'. Although the word continued to be used metaphorically in polite conversation as a description of status it became increasingly confined to those in full-time employment. Those who held offices under the Crown continued to describe themselves as the king's servants in the traditional sense, but the servants of a nobleman or gentleman would be those men and women who held positions in their employer's households. Such servants were not only dependent on their masters, they were also subject to him (or her) in a special sense, because the authority of a master over his household was an aspect of natural law. Such authority was not delegated by the king or dependent upon any statute, it was autonomous and *ex officio*. For this reasons, if a servant killed his master, his crime was not simply murder but petty treason. At the same time a master might strike his servant without committing an actionable offence. He had the legal right to administer 'reasonable chastisement' at his own discretion. However, that did not give him powers of life and death, as Lord Stourton discovered when he was hanged for murdering his gamekeeper.[7] This recognised authority extended in a number of directions. A master controlled not only his household servants, but also other employees such as journeymen or servants in husbandry with similar rights of chastisement. A schoolmaster or college tutor exercised the same rights in respect of his pupils, and many a nobleman's son bore the marks of his teacher's displeasure. Parents who committed their sons to such correction did not give specific permission for it to be exercised because it was a recognised part of the teacher's function.

The relationship between a man and his children, or a man and his wife, was similar. The patriarchal structures of scripture provided justification and many *exempla* for the exercise of such authority. On marriage a woman's property passed to her husband, who commonly retained a life interest in it if she predeceased him. She could not give evidence against him in a court of law, and was subject to his reasonable chastisement in the same manner as a servant. He was also entitled to the use of her body on demand, and no plea of rape was accepted within marriage. On the other hand she was entitled to be maintained by him, and he could not dispose of any of her property which he had acquired through marriage without her consent. The common law supported this customary authority and statute from time to time elaborated it but it did not create it. The head of a household needed no commission, and neither his wife nor any child under age could appeal against his jurisdiction except in matters of life and death. In practice, of course, this stark situation was frequently modified by the realities of kinship. When Mary Talbot, wife of the 6th Earl of Northumberland, wished to appeal against his harsh and insensitive treatment, she did not address herself to the king but to her father the Earl of Shrewsbury.[8] Many husbands of lesser rank must have been deterred from venting their anger on their wives by fear of their kindred. This was a protection unknown to the law, because in theory a woman abandoned her family when she took a husband, but in practice it was real, and frequently invoked. Children were more vulnerable, because they could have no such defence and we have no means of knowing what they may have suffered because such matters were not 'of record'. The canon law, even in its residual English form, was more likely to interest itself in family relationships than was the common law, which was mostly concerned with property. Adultery, fornication and incest, particularly the latter, were offences against the law of the Church, frequently investigated and often punished. Paedophilia was not known as such, but the sexual abuse of children by their own fathers was incest, and regarded with particular abhorrence. Women were more harshly treated than men by the law of adultery, because to a husband it could be grounds for divorce, but in theory offenders of both sexes were equally culpable. Marriage was a sacrament before it was a civil contract and both the secular and ecclesiastical courts were extremely reluctant to countenance its breakdown. Whether this was actually a protection to women or not may be debated but it was very hard for a man to escape from the responsibilities which marriage brought with it. Escape for a woman was easier, if that was what she wanted, but the consequent loss of her 'good name' was seldom a price worth paying in the culture of the sixteenth century.

The medieval authority of the Church had not only been sustained by Our Lord's original commission to St Peter, 'feed my sheep', which was deemed to have made the papacy the chief vehicle of divine jurisdiction, but also by the authority of the priestly order – *potestas ordinis*. The power to celebrate the sacraments of the Church, which derived from a priest's ordination, set him apart from the rest of the community. His power of absolution, and above all his ability to perform the miracle of the mass, placed him in an intercessory role between God and man. At best, this made him uniquely effective as a provider of religious consolation. He could assure the penitent of divine forgiveness, comfort the bereaved with authority, and strengthen the dying against supernatural fears. At worst, it gave him an excellent opportunity to exploit the credulous and superstitious for his own profit. The church had always been plagued by that paradox. Without the *potestas ordinis* its discipline became voluntary, and based upon persuasion. With it, it could easily degenerate into a greedy and corrupt institution. The Protestant Reformation arose partly from a widespread conviction that such abuse had infected the whole organisation, and that only by removing the power of orders entirely could the primitive mission of the Church be restored. The Protestant churches did not abolish ordination, indeed most of them remained very concerned about it, but by discontinuing the mass and removing the sacramental status of absolution, they removed the priest's *ex officio* authority. The reformed minister or pastor might retain the power of excommunication, but he exercised it as the agent of the congregation.[9] He could still offer intercessory prayer on behalf of his flock, and it might be valued because of his skill or holiness of life but such prayer was no longer perceived as having a different status from that of a layman. Similarly the reformed doctrine of justification by faith alone removed the perception of spiritual progression after death, and hence the whole concept of purgatory which existed to provide a form of posthumous rehabilitation. It was no longer claimed that the prayers of the living could in any way benefit the souls of those already departed. In so far as this weakened the sense of communion between the living and the dead, it narrowed the spiritual focus of the Church, but it also removed the temptation to sell vicarious spiritual benefits, or to control the living by manipulating their consciences.

England did not become Protestant overnight, and many of the consequences of religious change only gradually became apparent to the majority of the population.[10] The English Reformation at first had nothing to do with the *potestas ordinis*. Henry VIII assumed the *potestas jurisdictionis* (or power of government) in 1535, thinking that the priestly and episcopal offices would continue as before. However, even within his own lifetime that was not entirely true. Purgatory was carefully eschewed by the first manual of orthodoxy, *The King's Book* of 1543,[11] and even before that the great pilgrimage shrines which had played such an important part in medieval piety had been dismantled. When Thomas Cranmer addressed the king at Edward VI's coronation in February 1547, he made it clear that he did not consider his consecration to give him any authority to direct the king's proceedings:

The bishops of Canterbury for the most part have crowned your predecessors and anointed them kings of this land; yet it was not in their power to receive or reject them, neither did it give them authority to prescribe them conditions to take or leave their crowns.[12]

Already it was clear that the clergy were the king's subjects in a sense which had never applied before, and that their traditional ability to evade or bypass the common law had been greatly eroded. Within five years the mass had disappeared, the seven sacraments had been reduced to two and the whole concept of priestly authority *ex opere operato* (or sufficient in itself) had been dismantled. Mary's reaction briefly restored some of those powers, but because of the way in which it was carried out the Marian Church continued to derive much of its authority from the statutes which had recalled it to life. For the clergy themselves the Catholic restoration, followed by the renewed Protestantism of the Elizabethan settlement, was of immense significance; but for the much slower religious metabolism of the laity the changes were less violent. Liturgies might appear and disappear overnight, images go and come and go again, but men usually remain the same. Over a generation or so the Anglican vicar took over from the Catholic priest with no clearly perceived change of function. To the despair of educated Protestants communion wafers and texts of scripture continued to be used for the same quasi-magical purposes as holy water and *agni dei*.[13] Only slowly did the perception of the vicar or rector as a man of divine authority ebb away, and even as it ebbed it was replaced. By the end of the century the parson was an agent of the Crown. Not only was he expected to make official pronouncements from his pulpit and to proclaim the latest moves in ecclesiastical policy, he was also expected to activate the Poor Law and to exhort his flock in the performance of their secular duties. Obedience had always been a religious principle, but never more so than when duty to God and the queen ran through the same channel.

If the Church had become a department of state by 1600, the same was not true of traditional corporations. A mayor and a court of aldermen might derive their authority from a charter granted by the Crown, but neither they nor the citizens under their charge saw them as royal officers. After 1536, the chartered boroughs were the only secular liberties of any significance but the large ones, particularly London, deployed considerable resources. The structures of urban authority were confused, perhaps deliberately, by the fact that such officers frequently performed two functions. In cities which were also counties, such as Norwich or Newcastle-upon-Tyne, the mayor and aldermen also constituted the commission of the peace. In that capacity they exercised delegated jurisdiction and were answerable to the Council. But in respect of the powers which they exercised *ex officio* they were autonomous and answerable, if anywhere, to the freemen of the city. Every borough had a Recorder, who was the chief law officer, appointed by and responsible to the corporation; but every county borough also had a sheriff, who was a royal officer. The easiest way to distinguish between the two types of jurisdiction is in relation to the pleas handled. Pleas of the Crown – that is, treasons, felonies and statutory misdemeanours – were handled by the sheriffs and justices of the peace, whereas private pleas relating to the citizenship and business or craft discipline were heard by the city, sitting by virtue of its charter. It was not unknown for the mayor and his brethren to be granted a commission of oyer and terminer, which gave them the same powers as the justices of assize. But that was usually a matter of convenience and not a recognition of the status of the city. Guilds and companies, like the boroughs themselves, had a recognised right to rule themselves in respect of their own 'mysteries' or professional expertise and that authority was deemed to be natural. A guild would impose its own discipline upon its members and no appeal lay beyond its jurisdiction. However, as the sixteenth century advanced and particularly after 1530, that autonomy began to be eroded. If parliament chose to legislate new standards for the making of kerseys or hats, the statute overrode all existing regulations or privileges.

This was symptomatic of a progressive shift in the perceived nature of authority, which by the early seventeenth century had brought about a major change in the nature of English society. When Shakespeare made Henry V lament the burdens of kingship he represented him as saying:

> Upon the king! Let us our lives, our souls,
> Our debts, our careful wives,
> Our children, and our sins, lay on the king.
> We must bear all.[14]

It is very unlikely that it would have occurred to the real Henry V
to make such a protest, because what the playwright was expressing
was the result of over a century of carefully considered Tudor
policy. The wide diffusion of natural and divine authority which
characterised medieval society, and in which the king was only one
power, albeit a major one, had been replaced by something much
closer to the omnicompetent modern state. Henry V regarded his
peers as his kindred and his companions in arms. They were his
subjects, certainly, but not in the same sense as the tailor or the
ploughman. The same laws applied to them, but in different ways,
and were differently enforced. It would not have occurred to him to
accept responsibility for poor relief, except as a personal duty of
charity, for the teaching and discipline of the Church, or for the
quality of broadcloths manufactured in Suffolk. Public authority
had steadily encroached upon private until by the end of the
sixteenth century the remaining exempt areas were largely confined
to the family and to corporations of a business or professional
nature. By the end of Henry VIII's reign no allegiance was valid
against the kings, and by the end of Elizabeth's reign in theory at
least, God spoke exclusively with the monarch's voice. However,
the appearance of absolutism which this might present to the
uniformed observer was highly misleading. It had been achieved
by merging with the authority inherent in the Commonwealth, not
by defeating or superseding it. The *dominium politicum et regale* was
alive and well. It was more institutionally focused than when
Fortescue had enunciated it, but equally resistant to the logic of
strict political philosophy. The partnership between Crown and the
political nation was dynamic and to some extent unstable – a fact
which James I failed to perceive – but it worked as long as certain
unwritten conventions were obeyed. It is my purpose in the pages
which follow to explore the nature of that partnership, and the
reasons why it worked.

Notes

1. *Certain Homilies appointed by the King's Majesty to be declared and read by all Parsons, Vicars or Curates every Sunday in their Churches where they have cure* (1547).
2. Sir John Fortescue, *De Laudibus Legum Anglie*, ed. S. B. Chrimes (1949); Fortescue, *The Governance of England*, ed. C. Plummer (Oxford, 1885).

3.   Elaborate cases were constructed against the Duke of Buckingham in 1521 and against Anne Boleyn in 1536. Only in a handful of cases was the 'short cut' procedure of an Act of Attainder resorted to, notably those of Elizabeth Barton in 1535 and Cromwell himself in 1540.

4.   It was laid down in the statute 1 Edward VI c. 2 that all ecclesiastical courts should be held in the king's name and dated by regnal years – an instruction repealed by 1 Mary st.2 c. 2.

5.   Elizabeth had been bastardised by the annulment of her mother's marriage to the king, and this had been confirmed by the second succession Act of 1536. By the third succession Act of 1543 she was restored to the order after Mary but neither was recognised as legitimate.

6.   Robert Crowley on the causes of Kett's Rebellion. See R. H. Tawney and Eileen Power, *Tudor Economic Documents*, vol. III (1924) pp. 57–60.

7.   Grafton's *Chronicle*, vol. II (1809) p. 555.

8.   E. W. Ives, *Anne Boleyn*, p. 207.

9.   Justification by faith alone precluded the clergy of the reformed churches from cutting a delinquent off from the hope of salvation. Excommunication thus became a social sanction.

10.   On this gradualness, and the resistance which it implied, see particularly C. Haigh, *English Reformations* (1993), and Eamon Duffy, *The Stripping of the Altars* (1992).

11.   T. A. Lacey (ed.), *The King's Book* (1932) p. 164.

12.   J. E. Cox (ed.) *Cranmer's Miscellaneous Writings* (1846) p. 126.

13.   K. Thomas, *Religion and the Decline of Magic* (1971) pp. 72–4.

14.   *Henry V*, Act IV, Scene 1.

2 Structures

In principle all land in England belonged to the king. There had been allodial land before the Norman Conquest, as there was in most parts of Europe, but the fact of conquest had enabled William I to take everything into his own hands. Thereafter the bulk of the land had been dispersed upon a variety of tenures both military and civil. The commonest form of tenure was in chief by knight service, wherein the tenant swore homage and fealty to the king, was bound to attend him with a given number of armed men when summoned, and provided such counsel and advice as might be requested. Tenancies-in-chief were normally described as honours, and several honours might be grouped into a barony, but the terminology was imprecise. Except in border areas of the north and Wales, William and his successors made it their policy not to group honours into large consolidated estates, which might give their holders control over whole provinces. A tenant-in-chief was linked directly to the king, not only by the service which he was bound to perform, but also by the feudal 'incidents' which arose from his tenure. The most important of these was wardship, whereby if a vassal should die leaving his heir under age, control of that heir, and of the estate, passed to the king until the age of majority had been reached. This not only produced profit for the Crown, but was also a valuable means of social and political control. Tenancies-in-chief were almost invariably sub-infeudated, creating for the lord an affinity of his own vassals. In France by the late eleventh century this had already created serious problems for the Crown, when the sub-vassals' principal allegiance was to his lord rather than to the king. William had reduced this risk in England, partly by scattering honours and partly by requiring all sub-vassals to swear an additional oath of fealty to himself – the so-called 'oath of Salisbury'.

Land held by knight service was normally subject to escheat; that is to say, if the tenant died without heirs, his land reverted to his overlord. This made estates available for regrant, and regularly brought new families into the system. However land granted to a corporation did not escheat, and the fashionable practice of granting land to ecclesiastical foundations effectively took it out of circulation for the foreseeable future. This was known as 'mortmain', and had been curbed by statute as early as the thirteenth century.[1] Partly because mortmain required a royal licence, and partly because religious fashions had changed, large grants to the church had virtually ceased by the fifteenth century. The great monasteries never really recovered from the Black Death, and the *opus dei*, or constant fountain of prayer and praise which had provided the main inspiration for the monastic movement, had lost a lot of its popular appeal. The mendicant orders were popular, but neither desired nor attracted large endowments. By 1450 a rich man wishing to invest in his spiritual future was more likely to found a perpetual chantry; and by 1500 the fashion had shifted again to schools and university colleges. Such institutions were no less corporate and immortal than religious houses, but their lands were much less extensive than those of Glastonbury Abbey, or Fountains, and were perceived as being a social as well as a spiritual investment. One of the reasons why Henry VIII was able to dissolve the monasteries with comparatively little protest or resistance was because his action released onto the market a great quantity of land for which there was an overwhelming demand. The middle years of the sixteenth century saw the greatest property redistribution since the Norman Conquest. By the time that happened military tenure was almost entirely fictitious. Feudal incidents still existed, but the services had been commuted into rents which were almost indistinguishable from normal leases, and estates had become so fragmented that it was quite usual for a tenure in knight's service to be by the fortieth part of a knight's fee.

Not all land was held on tenure, military or otherwise, because many estates had from the beginning remained in the king's hands. Collectively these were known as the royal demesnes, and included castles and towns, forests and wastes, as well as pasture and tillage. Demesne lands might be farmed or managed directly by bailiffs, stewards or keepers appointed by the king, or they might be leased out for a term of years or lives. The demesne was one of the main sources of the king's revenue, but it fluctuated greatly in size and profitability from one generation to another. Augmented by escheats and by the consequences of attainder and forfeiture, it was as regularly diminished by new grants. Henry VI had been unable to refuse the demands of his servants and their friends, and so reduced his revenue that attempts were made to remedy the situation by Acts of Resumption. Henry VII by restrained patronage and much improved estate management raised his income from this source to over £40,000 a year, which was one of the secrets of his strength.[2]

By 1530 the bulk of the demesne revenue was accounted before the General Surveyors, shortly to become the court of that name, although feudal incidents and sheriffs' farms continued to be paid to the Exchequer. The ecclesiastical wealth acquired after 1536 was managed by the court of Augmentations, and became for the time being an extension of the royal demesne. However by 1547 more than half of it had been sold off or otherwise granted away, a process which brought in a sum in excess of £800,000.[3] By the reign of Elizabeth the royal demesne had returned to its early sixteenth-century scale, and if there had ever been any intention of a permanent large-scale augmentation, the opportunity had been lost. Elizabeth continued to sell land, especially when pressed by the exigencies of war, but the royal demesne remained a substantial social and economic factor long after the end of the sixteenth century.

The commonest unit of land management, whether in demesne or tenure, was the manor. A manor was a jurisdictional unit, not a topographical one. The fields of a single village might be divided between several manors, or a manor might contain several villages. Manors varied enormously in value and size, but they had one invariable characteristic in common – a group of tenants who formed the homage. The homage also constituted the manor court, which was conducted by the steward or bailiff in the name of the manorial lord.[4] If for any reason the homage disappeared, then the manor disappeared with it, for without a court there was only a seigneury. That could hardly happen by accident or natural misfortune, because even if the entire population was wiped out by plague, a new lord could replenish the homage from outside if he had the will to do so. A manor could only be destroyed by the will of the lord who, having obtained unity of possession, deliberately decided to maintain that situation. This happened with some frequency in the mid-fifteenth century, when the population level was low, many holdings were vacant, and sheep-ranching was becoming increasingly profitable. During the early sixteenth century, with the population increasing, unity of possession became much harder to achieve, and was proportionately more resented when it did occur. The land of every manor was divided, like England itself, into different functions. There was arable, pasture, woodland, waste and common. Waste and common were open to lord and homage alike, in accordance with locally determined customs of use. Arable, pasture and woodland were divided into demesne and tenurial land. Whether the lord farmed his demesne himself or not was irrelevant. The land could be leased out in ways which made it appear indistinguishable from tenurial land, but its legal status remained distinct.

Manorial tenancies were held by custom, and were servile in origin. The original homage would have been mainly villein, that is, personally unfree and unable to sue or be sued in the king's courts. By the sixteenth century personal unfreedom had become extremely rare, and where it existed was often unacknowledged. Customary tenancies were almost invariably held by freemen, often of gentle birth. That did not, however, affect the status of the land. The tenants normally held by copyhold, which meant that their right was registered on the roll of the manor court, of which they held a copy. That right was unrecognised by the common law, and could not be pleaded outside the manor. That did not necessarily mean that it was insecure, because the status of custom was universally recognised, but it did make tenants reluctant to oppose their lords, in whose name the customary court was held. In certain circumstances appeal could lie to the honour court of the overlord, which was equally a customary court, or to the king's equity jurisdiction in Chancery. But both of these were difficult and potentially expensive operations. Occasionally unscrupulous lords attempted to destroy the records of their own courts, but abuse of full copyhold was very seldom successful.[5] A much more common problem, and one very hard to remedy in a manorial court, arose when the lord deliberately exploited the waste or common land far beyond his entitlement. What constituted fair use was largely a matter of opinion, and in the absence of clearly defined constraints the homage was in a weak position to defend its interests. At the same time lords themselves were vulnerable to custom in a different way, because it was not only tenancy and usage rights which were so defined. Rents, entry fines and other dues had been similarly determined, often in the remote past. As long as prices remained stable or declining, as had been the case throughout the fifteenth century, everyone could be fairly relaxed about that situation.

However, when inflationary pressures began to be noticeable in the third and fourth decades of the sixteenth century, tension resulted. At first lords found their real income declining, and were unable to take remedial action because most of their tenancies had many years to run. Later, as tenancies became due for renewal, manorial courts attempted to insist on continuing the traditional rates. Quarrels were frequent and feelings ran high, with neither side enjoying a monopoly of rectitude. The sheer bother of having to struggle with the homage every time an obsolete due had to be increased drove some lords to attempt unity of possession who might not otherwise have contemplated such a course.

Although all land belonged ultimately to the king, the manorial system was not universal. Land might be held by freehold lease, which was protected by the common law, or by the ancient tenure of free socage. When the first colonies were established in the New World, the land there was equally assumed to belong to the Crown, and was granted in free socage 'as of the manor of East Greenwich'. The importance of all these tenurial arrangements in the English, or colonial, context was social and economic rather than political. The grant of a manor, or of an honour, or even of a number of honours, carried no jurisdictional rights other than the customary rights relating to the land itself. No great estate, whether honour or barony, was a unit of royal government, and no title of nobility carried with it *ex officio* jurisdictional powers. The king's government was therefore entirely separate from the pattern of land-holding, in marked contrast to most of central and western Europe, where it was normal for lands held of the Crown to carry with them the rights of the High Justice, the Middle and the Low.

The principal unit of government in England was the shire. Each shire had originally been governed in the king's name by an officer called the shire reeve, or sheriff. The sheriff had presided over the county court, returned all royal writs issued into his county, collected the revenues of the king's lands and the profits of the royal jurisdiction, and led the king's tenants in the event of a military summons.[6] It had been a key office of considerable prestige and power. By the sixteenth century it was much diminished, partly because of long term shifts in the pattern of royal administration, and partly because of the abuse to which it had been subjected during the Wars of the Roses. The county court, originally a popular court of the common law attended by all the freemen of the shire, had gradually lost the majority of its functions to the assizes and the quarter sessions. By 1500 it did very little except elect the knights of the shire to parliament. Sheriffs still accounted to the Exchequer for their 'farm' of royal revenues, but by the middle of the century these amounted to very little, as most of the money was passing through the hands of the receivers of the courts of General Surveyors and Augmentations. Although these courts were merged into the Exchequer in 1554, the receivers remained, and there was no return to the 'ancient course'. Two other officers assisted the sheriff in specific ways. The escheator ensured that the king's rights were prosecuted whenever there was a default of heirs, and the coroner conducted inquests upon unexpected or suspicious deaths. By 1550 escheators had been largely superseded by the feodaries of the court of wards, who performed the same function, and coroners were elected in the county court. Sheriffs still returned writs, and empanelled juries, which could be politically sensitive work in a local context.[7] Until the reign of Edward VI they also retained their role in mustering and commanding the county militia, but from 1551 onwards this was transferred to the newly created office of Lord Lieutenant. These lieutenants were normally noblemen, and the actual work fell to their deputies, but the sheriff lost what had originally been one of his most important responsibilities.[8] None of this diminished the importance of the county as a unit of local government, or reduced the determination of the monarch to remain in control. As new agencies were developed, the old ones gradually fell into disuse, but they did not disappear because they carried fees and perquisites, and because they represented to their holders a status which they would have been reluctant to relinquish.

Shires were divided into units as ancient as they were themselves. In some places these were called wapentakes, and in others rapes, but the normal name was hundred. Hundreds had originally been important units, but by the sixteenth century the hundred court had become even more moribund than the county court, and the high constable's duties were entirely formal. Unlike the counties, the hundreds created little sense of local identity, but they were useful units for assessment and muster purposes. Hundreds were in turn divided into parishes. The parish was an ecclesiastical rather than a civil unit, so the fit was not always perfect, but it had the great advantage of being a real community. The parish had no court, but its constable, although often pressed reluctantly into service, was a man of some substance whose local knowledge and influence was often of great value to the law enforcement officers.[9] After the establishment of the royal supremacy the incumbents and churchwardens of parishes were given increasing responsibilities for such matters as poor relief and the maintenance of roads and bridges. When enquiries were conducted in 1517, and again in 1548, to ascertain the extent and effect of enclosure since the beginning of Henry VIII's reign, a jury was empanelled from each parish to testify, and it was not unusual for a parish to maintain a small armoury from which men could be equipped at communal expense when they were summoned to military service.[10] In most respects the structure of royal government in the counties and their sub-divisions had proved remarkably successful in resisting 'privatisation', except during the dark days of the 1450s, and only the very minor royal courts called leets had passed into the hands of local lords. However by the sixteenth century the whole traditional structure was being rapidly superseded by new officers and new courts based upon the flexible and omnicompetent device of the royal commission.

The administration of the common law was controlled by the central courts of Common Pleas and King's Bench at Westminster. However these were seldom courts of first instance, because all cases had to be initiated, and most were heard, in the county in which the offence had been committed. Cases could be called to Westminster by writ of *nisi prius*, but by far the commonest role which the justices of the benches performed in regional law enforcement was as judges of assize. The assize circuits had gradually taken over from the General Eyre in the late thirteenth and fourteenth centuries. By the Tudor period the justices visited each county in England twice a year, hearing treasons, felonies and major property disputes. They operated by virtue of a commission of oyer and terminer, and they had the great advantage from the government's point of view of not being local men. However two sessions a year were not adequate, and since the fourteenth century the assizes had been supplemented by quarter sessions. For these the judges were not for the most part professional lawyers but gentlemen operating by virtue of a commission of the peace. At the beginning of the sixteenth century the competence of the assizes and quarter sessions was very similar, except that the assizes were more likely to deal with cases in which powerful local interests were involved. However as the century advanced treasons and major property issues were taken out of the hands of quarter sessions, and the referral of major felonies from the sessions to the Assizes became more common. Very few records survive from either of these types of court before the later sixteenth century. By the later part of Henry VIII's reign writs executed at the assizes were routinely returned to King's bench, but few assize rolls remain which would enable them to be usefully interpreted.[11]

The virtual disappearance of county and hundred courts also left a gap in the lower levels of law enforcement. Quarter sessions could deal with petty misdemeanours, but they only met for a few days at a time and had more important business to attend to. Consequently such cases tended to be dealt with at *ad hoc* meetings of two or more justices of the peace, which were known as petty sessions. Such sessions could not touch life or real property, and were summary in their nature, dealing out corporal punishment and small fines.

Except at this minor level the processes of the common law tended to be formal and elaborate. When a serious accusation was made, it had to be investigated. This would originally have been carried out by the sheriff or one of his deputies, but by the sixteenth century such police work normally fell to a justice of the peace. If there appeared to be a case, then a formal indictment would be drawn up and the offender, if not already in custody, arrested. The indictment was then presented to the grand jury of the county, either at assizes or quarter sessions, in order to be 'proved'. If the *prima facie* case was then confirmed, the indictment would be endorsed *billa vera* (true bill) and sent for trial. At this point the great majority of cases broke down, because the accused had already made good his escape and could not be tried in his absence. Recovering fugitives in these circumstances was immensely difficult, because no officer's jurisdiction extended beyond the limits of his county.[12] Once a wanted person had crossed the county boundary, a fresh search had to be initiated in the neighbouring shire. A fugitive's goods could be distrained, and he or she could eventually be declared an outlaw. This might prove effective against a person of some substance, who had a family interest to protect, but against the poor or rootless it was normally useless. If the offence was treason then the king's Council might override the limitations of county jurisdiction and issue a warrant for the arrest of the offender wherever he might be found but that would not be done in the case of ordinary felonies. In the late fourteenth century less than 20 per cent of indictments had resulted in trials.[13] The Tudor record was probably somewhat better, but the severity of the law's punishments reflected the low risk of conviction. In civil cases the common law was relatively effective, and the security of its recorded judgments was greatly appreciated, but the king's peace had to be preserved by other means. At the beginning of the sixteenth century several parts of England and the whole of Wales stood wholly or partly outside the shire system. The two parts of the principality of Wales, administered from Caernarfon and Carmarthen were divided into units called counties, which had sheriffs, but no commissions of the peace or parliamentary representation. They also had a different court system and were not visited by the justices of assize. Eastern Wales, along the English border, was still divided into marcher lordships. Many of these had long since fallen to the crown, but they had no county structure and their courts operated in the name of the marcher lord. These courts administered both the English common law and certain aspects of Welsh customary law. In spite of all efforts these lordships remained notoriously turbulent, and in 1536 the whole antique system was abolished by statute.

The two Acts of 1536 and 1543 redefined the principality to include not only the traditional apanages, but also those parts of Wales previously administered by the marcher lords, or under the supervision of the prince's Council. The whole of Wales was divided into twelve shires on the English model. Commissions of the peace were introduced and each county was given one representative in the House of Commons. Quarter sessions were established and the use of Welsh law discontinued, but the existing common law courts, called the courts of Great Session, were reorganised and did not become dependent upon Westminster.[14] In the north of England the palatine bishopric of Durham also stood apart. The palatinate was not coextensive with the bishop's ecclesiastical jurisdiction, which also covered Northumberland, nor with his estates, which occupied only part of the county. Durham was unique in that it seemed to be a normal shire, with a sheriff and commission of the peace. However both these functioned in the name of the bishop rather than the king, and no members were sent to parliament. In 1536 the bishop's nominal control was removed, and all writs ran thereafter in the king's name. The county was also brought within the assize system, but unlike the Welsh shires, no members were sent to Westminster until the later part of the seventeenth century.

Even further north other exempt jurisdictions existed along the Anglo-Scottish border. In the fifteenth century Tynedale and Redesdale were full liberties, governed by their wardens, but in 1495, in a move which created an important precedent for later legislation, they were absorbed into the county of Northumberland.[15] Northumberland was an odd county because its constant exposure to Scottish raids meant that its normal civilian government was constantly being interrupted, and had to co-exist uneasily with the military administration of the East March, centred on the fortress town of Berwick. A similar relationship existed between the county of Cumberland and the West March, centred on Carlisle, but Cumberland was less troubled than its more accessible eastern neighbour. There were other parts of England with distinctive jurisdictional features, the Earldom of Chester, for example, or the Cinque Ports, but these no longer had the functions of liberties by the late fifteenth century, and remained as more or less inconsequential anachronisms for some time to come.

Urban government was not in any proper sense franchisal. The exact relationship between a chartered borough and the county within which it was situated depended upon the specific terms of its charter. All disputes concerned with the conduct of business within the town were normally privileged. The mayor and his brethren were responsible for the assessment and collection of taxation. Sometimes towns were mustered separately and sometimes as part of the county. This varied not only between one town and another, but between one period and another in respect of the same town.[16] Not infrequently there were disputes. Most boroughs grew out of royal manors, and received their charters of incorporation from the Crown. Some had been created by lay or ecclesiastical lords for their own purposes. By the sixteenth century only the Crown was issuing charters, and during the middle years of the century a deliberate policy was pursued which resulted in about thirty new creations between 1547 and 1558. The reason for this seems to have been a conviction that civil order and discipline were best maintained by privileged groups defending their own interests. Burgesses were notoriously conservative in their sense of social hierarchy, and their presence in significant numbers within a county helped to soften the sharp dichotomy between gentry and commons which had been so obvious in the turmoils of 1549. However this discipline was a question of police work, not jurisdiction. Except for the county boroughs, which had their own officers, all corporate towns were subjected to the county quarter sessions and assizes without differentiation. Mayors could neither issue nor return writs, although they were responsible for the conduct of all elections within their boroughs, including those which sent the members to the House of Commons. Towns tended to be fiercely protective of their privileges, and aggressive in extending their control beyond their proper limits into their economic hinterland which provided a fruitful source of controversies with the county commissions.

Kings of England did not have a monopoly of divine authority but they did have a unique responsibility to provide good government, and like all medieval kings, they had originally discharged that responsibility through their households. However by the fourteenth century the strength of the common law and of the shire structure had enabled a number of the key aspects of government to move 'out of court' and become permanently located at Westminster. The Chancery – the office of the Lord Chancellor – was the original royal secretariat and the principal department of administration, controlling the Great Seal. By the fifteenth century it had lost most of its administrative functions to the Privy Seal but expanded greatly as a court of equity. Equity was the exercise of the king's right and duty to provide justice where the common law might be deficient for one reason or another. At the beginning of the Tudor period this might mean issues which fell uneasily between the common law and the canon law, issues where common law prosecution was ineffective because of the local power of the defendant, and issues for which the common law provided no remedy. Maritime issues which had once also been a matter of equity, were by the late fifteenth century handled by the court of the Lord Admiral.[17] Chancery business had expanded greatly since about 1450 by adjudicating cases arising from copyhold or unfree tenures on appeal from manor or honour courts, and by offering protection to the extra-legal procedure of enfeoffment to use, whereby testators sought to avoid a common law ban on devising estates by will. After 1485 the king's council provided remedy against over-mighty defendants, and after 1535 ecclesiastical issues were dealt with under the royal supremacy, but

the need to provide equitable supplements to the common law
continued to increase and diversify. Chancery also had a common
law side – a separate court – which provided remedy against the
king. Since no writ could run against the king and he could not be
sued it was necessary to provide for situations in which mistakes
had been made and acknowledged. The Chancery court did that
by accepting and processing petitions of right, in response to which
the king made voluntary restitution.

The second out-of-court department, namely the Exchequer,
similarly had a number of different functions. It was originally
the chief revenue office of the Crown, and as such it had two
departments, the Lower Exchequer of Receipt and the Upper
Exchequer of Audit. The latter functioned substantially unchanged
for centuries, its complex procedures virtually proof against fraud,
but so arcane as to be impossible to use for budgetary calculations.
The Lower Exchequer only intermittently handled real money.
Much of the king's income had always been spent on assignment,
which meant that the Receipt obtained only the evidence of the
transaction, not actual cash. It was also normal for monarchs to use
their household spending departments, the Wardrobe or the
Chamber, to keep control of cash receipts, although it was again
usual for the accounts to go to the Exchequer. Consequently the
fact that the early Tudor Exchequer was not a real treasury
represented nothing new. It was the so-called restoration of the
'ancient course' in 1554 which provided the real change in financial
management, and the Elizabethan Exchequer, for all its deficien-
cies, was closer to being a national revenue department than
anything which had existed for a very long time. Disputes inevitably arose from the process of accountancy, and these were
resolved by a common law court attached to the Exchequer and
called the Exchequer Chamber. This was presided over by the
Treasurer of the Exchequer, assisted by the barons as judges.
During the sixteenth century the competence of this court steadily
expanded as it was perceived to offer a swifter and cheaper
alternative to the Common Pleas. After 1579 the barons of the
Exchequer had to be common lawyers, and were chosen, like all the
other judges of the two benches, from among the sergeants-at-law.

The third department, if it may be called that, which jostled for
elbow room in Westminster Hall, consisted of the ancient courts of
common law, the Common Pleas and the King's Bench. Of these

the latter was the more powerful and prestigious. It dealt with all pleas of the Crown which meant mostly criminal jurisdiction, and also heard pleas of error from all other common law courts.[18] The concept of appeal was unknown to the medieval common law, but a writ of error could be obtained to secure a retrial. This would only stand if a technical error of some kind could be proved in the original trial, but in cases where new evidence had come to light or manifest injustice had been done, such errors were remarkably easy to find. At the end of the fifteenth century King's Bench was in decline. It had not become finally fixed at Westminster until 1421, but once settled it had come to depend largely on cases summoned from the counties by writs of *certiorari* or *terminari*. Only pleas originating in Middlesex came to it of first instance. This situation had already produced some ingenious responses before the Tudor period began. The development of fictitious or collusive trespass actions to determine entitlement to real property (because it was impossible to trespass on your own land) and of trespass on the case to extend common law protection to victims of libel or slander (trespass on the reputation) were typical examples. Another was process by bill of Middlesex whereby a case might be brought within the jurisdiction of the court by pretending a fictitious custody of the defendant in the Marshalsea which was the prison of the court.[19]

By the late sixteenth century King's Bench had recovered strongly, largely at the expense of Common Pleas. Common Pleas was the oldest of the common law courts and handled all suits between party and party, which were overwhelmingly property disputes of one kind or another. During the fifteenth century it was the busiest and consequently the slowest and most expensive of the courts. In spite of this it continued to be popular because the alternatives were so unsatisfactory. Equity was not supposed to function in cases triable by the common law, unless there was evidence of intimidation. Informal processes of arbitration were often used but the decisions reached had no status in law should one party or the other subsequently become dissatisfied. The decisions of Common Pleas, on the other hand, were absolutely binding. The court declined during the sixteenth century, partly because of poaching by King's Bench, but more importantly because of the rise of a new and more effective kind of equity jurisdiction in the conciliar courts of Star Chamber and Requests.

The extension of common law jurisdiction into the counties came, as we have seen, via the assizes and quarter sessions. The assize judges were professional lawyers, usually justices of one or other of the benches, and they frequently heard on circuit cases which had been referred to them from Westminster. Nevertheless the assizes were not *ex officio* extensions of King's Bench and Common Pleas. There were six circuits, ridden twice a year, and the justices derived their authority from commissions of oyer and terminer and gaol delivery. In other words they were directly empowered by the king rather than being a part of a central bureaucratic structure. As such they formed a very important link between the centre and the localities, which helped to mitigate the increasing detachment between the royal prerogative and the common law. As recently as the 1470s Edward IV had occasionally presided in King's Bench himself, but by the reign of James I any direct involvement by the king was rejected as unacceptable, and that was not just the view of the abrasive Chief Justice Edward Coke.

Other aspects of the central administration which were not parts of the royal household were the Privy Seal office and the parliament. The latter was not so much an institution as an event, and we shall be considering its peculiar status and functions in due course. The Privy Seal had begun as the king's personal activator for the Great Seal, and it retained, in theory at least, an essential role in that chain of command. By the fifteenth century it had lost personal touch with the king, and had become a department under the Lord Privy Seal. As such it was the main clearing house for general administration, channelling business to other departments or to the household as appropriate. This it continued to do until the rise of the Secretary in the 1530s. Thereafter the Privy Seal continued to be used by the court of Requests, by the Privy Council until 1556, and for the specific purpose of authorising forced loan repayments, in addition to its general authenticating role.[20] As a department of any significance the day of the Privy Seal was over by 1540, and its putative successor, the signet office, never really got off the ground. Despite the spilling of much controversial ink, there was no consistent movement of administrative control either into or out of the household during the sixteenth century. The Council and its agencies became more formalised, but the Council itself remained directly answerable to the monarch. Administrative control moved into the household when the secretariat replaced the Privy Seal Office, but financial control went in the opposite direction when the treasury of the Chamber was replaced, first by the autonomous financial courts and then by a revitalised Exchequer. The revenue courts were originally four in number. One, First-Fruits and Tenths, was a direct result of the establishment of the royal supremacy, and a second, Augmentations, was an indirect result. The other two were developments from existing revenue offices, the courts of General Surveyors and Wards and Liveries. In 1547 the two land courts, Augmentations and General Surveyors, were merged. In 1554 this merged court was absorbed by the Exchequer and First-Fruits and Tenths was abolished with the royal supremacy which had called it into existence. When the supremacy was restored in 1559, the spiritual revenues were directed into an office of the Exchequer. Wards and Liveries survived as an independent department, and so also did the Duchy of Lancaster Chamber, which had provided the model for the accounting methods used in the short-lived courts, and subsequently taken over by the new Exchequer offices. The Exchequer was enlarged and modified to meet the new demands being made upon it, and financial control never reverted to any aspect of the household.[21]

Until 1534 the government of the church was, at least in theory, entirely independent. Its jurisdiction was answerable not to the king but to the papal Curia, and its law was the canon law of western Christendom. Strictly speaking there was no such thing as the *Ecclesia Anglicana*, but only the two autonomous provinces of Canterbury and York, each with its convocation and hierarchy of courts. In practice the king exercised a great deal of influence not only over senior ecclesiastical appointments, but also over the way in which each province conducted its business. Clerical subsidies, for example, were never as difficult to obtain as those from the laity and royal intrusions into matters of patronage were numerous at all ecclesiastical levels. It was never wise to ignore the king's wishes, when these were expressed, whatever the technical status of his intervention. Relations between Church and Crown were generally good between 1415 and 1525, because each derived strength from the support of the other. However the late fourteenth century statutes of Provisors and Praemunire had never been repealed, in spite of papal representations, and stood as a reminder that the king respected ecclesiastical liberties of his own goodwill. Each province was divided into sees, three in York and eighteen in Canterbury. These were the ecclesiastical equivalents of the secular counties, but were not coextensive with them. Each bishop was responsible for the discipline of his flock as well as for its pastoral care. His chief agents for that purpose were the archdeacons, each responsible for a part of the diocese and armed with a consistory court. Both bishops and archdeacons were supposed to carry out regular visitations of an inquisitorial nature and the records of their investigations form one of the richest sources for the social history of the period. Archdeaconries were divided into rural deaneries, and they in turn into parishes which were the units within which most ordinary Christians lived out their lives. This apparently simple structure was in practice shot through with numerous exceptions and anomalies. The most obvious were the communities of the regular religious, some of whom were subject to episcopal visitation, but many were not, being answerable only to the provincial of their own order. Usually such officials were located within England but not invariably so. Some churches for historical reasons were also 'peculiars', exempt from the jurisdiction of their immediate super-iors. There had for centuries been a controversial boundary between secular and ecclesiastical jurisdictions, epitomised by the long-running issue over criminous clerks. Such disputes were inevitable while the Church held substantial landed endowments, and controlled sensitive areas such as probate and contract. The generally good relations prevailing at the end of the fifteenth century enabled Henry VII to cut down rights of sanctuary and restrict benefit of clergy without any serious repercussions, but no amount of goodwill could avail Henry VIII a generation later when he wished to escape from the pope's matrimonial jurisdiction. The fracas over the King's Great Matter which resulted in the declaration of the royal supremacy totally changed the jurisdic-tional status of the Church. All those ultimate powers which had been exercised by the pope now fell to the king. The *Ecclesia Anglicana* became a reality, which could be legislated for. The bishops and heads of religious houses took the oath of Supremacy, and an unpleasant fate awaited the few who refused.

The administrative structure of the church, however, did not change at all. The religious houses were soon swept away, leaving a few more jurisdictional anomalies, but the basic structure of bishoprics, archdeaconries and parishes, of consistory courts and

cathedral chapters, remained unchanged. Remarkably, these institutions survived not only the royal supremacy but also the onset
of Protestantism. Partly for that reason there never developed a
central administrative office for the government of the Church.
Although it would be in many ways correct to describe the
Elizabethan Church as a department of state for ecclesiastical
affairs, the Archbishop of Canterbury never sat in Westminster
Hall. Henry's brief experiment of appointing Thomas Cromwell as
Viceregent in Spirituals was not repeated, and the nearest thing
there ever was to a central institution was the court of High
Commission. The Archbishop of Canterbury was a royal servant,
and the Church became an integral part of the framework of royal
government but it was not controlled by its own institutions.
Parliament legislated for it, and it was run by the monarch and
Council – in other words from within the household.

   The royal household, or court, was the hub and focus of all
political life and became increasingly dominant as the great noble
households slowly withered under the pressure of Tudor policy.
Somewhat confusingly the household proper, the domain of the
Lord Steward, was not politically important. It consisted of the
service department – kitchen, buttery, scullery and so on, managed
by the Counting House, or Board of Greencloth. Only a handful of
the 200-odd servants who staffed these departments were gentlemen. The household 'below stairs' had its own career structure and
a very high degree of stability.[22] Patronage within it theoretically
belonged to the Lord Steward or the Controller, but in practice was
mainly exercised by the departmental sergeants. The politically
significant parts of the Court were the Chamber and the Privy
Chamber. Theoretically the Lord Chamberlain was responsible for
both, but by the middle years of Henry VIII's reign the latter
enjoyed virtual autonomy under the Chief Gentleman. The Privy
Chamber was not in any sense an institution of government.

   It began in the 1490s as a group of personal, and even menial,
servants who attended to the king's immediate needs. It was
essentially private and was designed to give Henry VII a screen
of privacy behind which to seek relief from the unremittingly public
nature of his normal routine. His son needed no such screen, and
quickly turned the Privy Chamber into a club for his boon
companions, mostly young nobles and gentlemen who shared his
boisterous tastes in music and physical exercise. By 1520 these

'mignons' were officially designated 'Gentlemen of the Privy Chamber' on the French model.[23] Their constant uncontrolled access to the king gave them great influence, and they became much in demand as intermediaries and intercessors. The king used his gentlemen as personal envoys to conduct delicate negotiations both within the realm and abroad and it has been claimed that in the latter years of Henry's reign the Privy Chamber rivalled the Privy Council in power. During these years the Privy Purse, held by the Chief Gentleman, expanded from being a pocket-money account into a significant spending department handling tens of thousands of pounds, and exempt from normal accounting controls. The staff of the Privy Chamber numbered between twenty and forty, including grooms and lesser servants. The gentlemen did not usually hold offices of any importance while they served in the Privy Chamber, and they had no formal responsibility to offer the King advice or to execute his decisions.

The great days of the Privy Chamber ended with Henry VIII's death. The Earl of Warwick, Edward VI's second regent, was careful to reconstruct its personnel in order to ensure his own ascendancy and that of his friends over the rapidly developing king. A few of the gentlemen appointed after 1550 appear to have been Edward's personal choice but there was by that time significant overlap of membership with the Privy Council, and there was no chance of serious rivalry between the two.[24] On the other hand the King's Privy Coffers continued to handle large sums of money, and it appears that preparations were already in hand to deliver them to Edward's personal management in the months before he died.[25] Had the king achieved his majority and assumed full control of the government, no doubt the Privy Chamber would have recovered its former importance. His death changed the whole situation. The last two Tudors were women, and their personal attendants and companions were naturally female. Convention would have ensured that, even if preference did not. Almost overnight the Privy Chamber became a glorified boudoir, and its political importance almost disappeared. Almost but not quite. The Emperor Charles V feared, probably without justification, that Mary's ladies exercised far too much influence over her; and Elizabeth allowed her judgement in matters such as promotions and patronage to be influenced by a Privy Chamber which consisted largely of the wives and daughters of her councillors and ministers.

The Privy Chamber was a relatively small and intimate group, the importance of which rested upon its close and uninterrupted relationship with the monarch. The Great Chamber was a much larger and more amorphous organisation, but was in many respects closer to being an instrument of government. It was in the Great Chamber that the officers of the court and the chief officers of state kept their tables upon formal occasions and it was as members of the Chamber that Privy Councillors were entitled to bouge of court. The Council normally met at court, in a room allocated for the purpose in that part of the palace controlled by the Lord Chamberlain. Equally important, the Chamber was a large and flexible centre of patronage and communication. There was an insatiable demand for positions at court, not because they carried large fees, which they did not, but because they were honourable and represented attractive opportunities for profitable networking. In order to satisfy this demand Henry VIII worked his gentlemen sewers and ushers, and his gentlemen pensioners, in shifts, eventually quadrupling the number who were needed at any given time. Gentle families from every county of England and Wales were represented in Chamber service between 1540 and 1547. Often rival families from the same county intrigued at court to secure advantages over their rivals, and to be unrepresented was considered to be a serious disadvantage in local politics. It would probably be no exaggeration to say that the Chamber constituted an informal but effective mechanism for the management of county power structures, just as the court of Wards gave the Crown intermittent but invaluable leverage against the nobility. In the early sixteenth century the Treasury of the Chamber was also the king's principal revenue department. That came to an end with the rise of Thomas Cromwell, but Cromwell had no particular aversion to the use of the Chamber for political purposes. Not only did he exert himself to control patronage and appointments, he also made sure that the senior household officers retained their places *ex officio* when the Privy Council was reorganised. The king's secretary was not an officer of the Chamber any more than the Lord Privy Seal, but the nature of his personal responsibility to the king brought him within its compass. If the Privy Council was an aspect of the court, as it surely was, then the secretary was a household officer. As long as the monarch remained his, or her, own chief executive then the government of the realm was bound to remain focused in the court, and that meant within the broadly defined and flexible embrace of the Chamber. There ambassadors were entertained and the theatre of the monarchy acted out its dramas. It was the Chamber rather than the Privy Chamber or Westminster Hall, which was the vehicle of Tudor *maiestas* and the place where aspiring courtiers skirmished for attention and opportunities.

Notes

1. In 1279. See *Statutes of the Realm* ed. A. Luders *et al.*, 11 vols, 1810–28 vol. I, pp.26–100.
2. B. P. Woolfe, *The Crown Lands, 1461–1536* (1970) p. 69.
3. The gross receipts from land sales totalled £799,310 between 1536 and 1547, but jewels and plate seized realised another £80,000, and the total derived from former monastic property was probably in the region of £1.3 million. See J. A. Guy, *Tudor England* (1988) p. 145.
4. For a succinct and helpful account of manorial constitutions, see E. Kerridge, *The Agrarian Problem in the Sixteenth Century and After* (1969).
5. Ibid.
6. Sir Thomas Smith, *De Republica Anglorum* ed. M. Dewar (Cambridge, 1982) pp. 96–8.
7. A succession of statutes attempted to control unsatisfactory juries throughout the century: 11 Henry VII cs 24, 25; 23 Henry VIII c. 3; 26 Henry VIII c. 4; 32 Henry VIII c. 9; 5 Elizabeth c. 9; 27 Elizabeth c. 6.
8. G. S. Thomson, *Lords Lieutenant in the Sixteenth Century* (1923).
9. J. Youings, *Sixteenth-Century England* (1984) p. 121; Smith, *De Republica Anglorum*, pp. 109–1109.
10. R. W. Hoyle (ed.), *The Military Survey of Gloucestershire, 1522* (1993) p. 1.
11. M. Blatcher, *The Court of King's Bench 1450–1550* (1978).
12. J. G. Bellamy, *Crime and Public Order in England in the Later Middle Ages* (1973) pp. 89–120.
13. Ibid., pp. 1–35; D. Loades, *Politics and the Nation, 1450–1660* (1992) p. 30.
14. Statute 34 & 35 Henry VIII c. 26; *Statutes of the Realm*, vol. III, p. 926. Glanmor Williams, *Wales and the Act of Union* (1992) pp. 32–3. Four circuits of Great Sessions were established, covering Caernarfon, Merionydd and Anglesey; Flint, Denbigh, and Montgomery; Glamorgan, Brecon and Radnor; and Pembroke, Carmarthen and Cardigan. Monmouth was attached to the English assize circuit of Oxford.
15. Statute 11 Henry VII, c. 9.
16. L. O. Boynton, *The Elizabethan Militia* (1967) pp. 13–50.
17. M. J. Pritchard and D. E. C. Yale, *Hale and Fleetwood on Admiralty Jurisdiction* (Selden Society, 1993), pp. xxix–xxxviii.
18. W. S. Holdsworth, *A History of the English Law*, vol. I, ed. S. B. Chrimes (1956) pp. 35ff., 204ff.

19. M. Blatcher, 'Touching the writ of Latitat; an Act "of no great moment" ', in *Elizabeth Government and Society*, S. T. Bindoff, J. Hurstfield and C. H. Williams (eds) (1961) pp. 188ff.
20. G. R. Elton, *The Tudor Constitution* (1982) p. 118.
21. G. R. Elton, *The Tudor Revolution in Government* (1953) pp. 117ff., 255ff.
22. D. Loades, *The Tudor Court* (Bangor, 1992) pp. 59–72.
23. D. Starkey 'Intimacy and innovation: the rise of the Privy Chamber, 1485–1547' in *The English Court from the Wars of the Roses to the Civil War* (1987) pp. 71–118.
24. J. A. Murphy, 'The illusion of decline: the Privy Chamber, 1547–1558', in *The English Court* ed. D. Starkey (1987) p. 133.
25. D. E. Hoak, 'The secret history of the Tudor Court: the King's Coffers and the King's purse, 1542–1553', *Journal of British Studies*, 26 (1987).

3 The Council

The chief executive and administrative instrument of the Crown was the Council. This had existed in one form or another since the origins of the monarchy itself, and consisted of a group of men appointed, in theory at least, entirely at the king's discretion. In practice the choice had not always been entirely free, because no king could afford to exclude all his most powerful nobles, or allow the Church to be unrepresented. The representation of different interest groups was a matter of common sense rather than prescription, and tended to be argued most strongly during periods of royal weakness. Between 1445 and 1455 the Duke of York, Henry VI's most powerful subject, and until 1453 his heir, had been confronted by a Council consistently hostile to him. Henry allowed, and indeed encouraged, his favourites, first the Duke of Suffolk and then the Duke of Somerset, to exercise such control over the Council that York was excluded. Duke Richard and his friends then began to argue that his proximity to the Crown, and the extent of his affinity, entitled him to a seat at the Council board, irrespective of the king's wishes – that he was what they began to call a 'councillor born'.[1] York's relationship with Henry thereafter rested upon force rather than law or custom, and no general conclusions can be drawn from it. When York's son Edward became king in 1461, he could hardly have dispensed with the services of his chief supporter, Richard Neville, Earl of Warwick. But after his break with Neville had resulted in rebellion and the brief loss of his crown in 1470–1, no other councillor enjoyed a similar influence. Edward consulted his magnates as he chose, some regularly, some occasionally, and some not at all, in accordance with their availability and his judgement of their usefulness. His most important councillors tended to be bishops such as Rotheram of York and Morton of Ely, but lesser nobles of his own creation, such as Hastings, Dinham and Mountjoy, also featured prominently, as did lesser clerics and knights such as Sir John Fogge and Sir William Parr. Although he called over one hundred men to Council in the course of his reign, an average meeting consisted of no more than ten or twelve, of whom the majority were always officers of state or household.

Like his predecessors, Edward also made occasional use of an extended body called the Great Council. This was always summoned for a particular purpose: in February 1476 to approve the new regulations for the Calais wool staple, and in the following year to advise the king on relations with Burgundy following the death of his brother-in-law Charles the Bold.[2] The composition of the Great Council seems to have varied in accordance with the king's wishes. Sometimes it was an augmented meeting of the ordinary Council, and sometimes every peer was summoned by individual writ as for a parliament. There seem to have been no rules, or even customs, governing these assemblies, and the status of the advice which they offered was the same as that of the ordinary Council; the king accepted it or ignored it at his pleasure. When summoned by writ the Great Council did enjoy a corporate identity, but it did not exercise any collective responsibility. The ordinary Council, although it was a standing body, did not have a corporate identity, and was equally lacking in collective responsibility, in which it differed completely from a modern cabinet. Each councillor was sworn individually to the king, to advise in accordance with his own knowledge and conscience. No attempt was made to manufacture a consensus, and most monarchs welcomed conflicting advice, because it gave them a wider perspective upon the problem in question, and the greatest possible freedom of choice. The Council only made decisions in its administrative capacity. As an executive it carried out policy for which the monarch was solely responsible, and as an advisory body it was almost entirely reactive. The Council also exercised a quasi-judicial function. It was not a court of law, but it did process petitions and complaints addressed to the king. Often these were simply passed to the most appropriate court, with a covering admonition in the king's name to see justice speedily and effectively executed. Sometimes, however, the Council arbitrated itself. This might happen if the law provided no remedy and the case was not deemed appropriate for the Chancery, but the procedure was more frequently used when the parties were powerful lords, and the king's peace might be endangered by delay. In other words the Council, or some designated part of it, acted as a court of equity. As such it was an agent of the king's prerogative, and its authority derived entirely from the Crown.

The Council was thus a multifaceted body, and pursued its different agendas in different ways. Formal meetings followed the law terms, were normally held in the palace of Westminster, and were somewhat sparsely minuted by a clerk appointed for the purpose. Judicial arbitrations, and certain kinds of administrative business, were only discharged at such meetings. However executive action, let alone advice to the monarch, could not be constrained by such a timetable. Councillors accompanied the king wherever he went, or at least wherever he was acknowledged to have gone, and were on hand whenever business was to be transacted. Such councillors varied in numbers and seniority, and the only criterion of attendance was the king's pleasure. Whether the Council could be said to be 'attendant' upon the king in such circumstances was a matter of opinion. There were no formal or recorded meetings, but informal consultations were frequently held, often in the king's presence, which was not normally the case with minuted sessions.

Henry VII took over this institution from his predecessor, and a surprising large proportion of its personnel. No fewer than 29 of his councillors had served either Edward or Richard, and nineteen of them had recently been sworn to the man whom he had just defeated and killed as a usurper.[3] One of the reasons for this was that the followers who had returned with him out of exile were few and lacking in political experience. Another was his desire to put the past to rest, and to reconcile the feuds which the wars between York and Lancaster had generated. Loyalty to himself, and the ability to serve, were the essential criteria for membership of Henry's Council. Over the full 24 years of his reign some 227 councillors have been identified, but of those 44 did not attend any recorded meeting. In their case the use of the term may have been honorific; they may have been specialist advisers who would only have been called on very occasionally; or there may have been a significant number of meetings of which no record survives. Of the 183 who are known to have attended, 43 were peers and 61 churchmen. The balance was made up of non-noble courtiers, lawyers and officials in approximately equal numbers. This balance was very similar to that achieved by Edward, but is slightly misleading in the sense that it did not remain constant throughout the reign. The proportion of nobles and ecclesiastics dropped slightly after 1500 in favour of lawyers and officials, but the shift was not dramatic. More important was regularity of attendance, and in that respect the courtiers and officials enjoyed a clear ascendancy. The average attendance at recorded meetings was well below twenty, and the number of active councillors at any given time was probably around two dozen. A large proportion of these were senior officials – the Lord Chancellor, Lord Treasurer, Lord Privy Seal, Lord Chamberlain, and a few others. No attempt was ever made to gather the whole Council together at one time, and no useful purpose would have been served by such a gathering. If a broad basis of consent was needed, a parliament was more effective, and better understood.

The procedures of Henry's Council, like its composition, were continuous with the past. Formal meetings were held in the law terms, and informal meetings whenever and wherever convenient. However, subtle shifts of emphasis can be discerned which were to be significant for the future. There were references to the Council attendant, as distinct from the Council at Westminster. It used to be thought that this signified the development of distinct standing groups or committees within the Council, but it is now recognised that the terminology was much more casual than that would imply, merely signifying those councillors who happened at any given moment to be in one place or the other. The same applies to the notorious 'Council Learned in the Law'. Although this group had a clearly defined function, it was not a clearly defined group, consisting simply of such legally trained councillors as happened to be available at any given time.[4] The regular participation of Sir Richard Empson and Edmund Dudley reflected the fact that they were normally employed about that sort of business, not that the 'Council Learned' had been set up to support them. The concept of a Council committee, with an established membership and a regular reporting procedure, had not yet evolved.[5] For the same reason the idea of an 'inner' and an 'outer' Council also needs to be treated with extreme caution. Henry inevitably consulted some advisers, and used some agents, far more frequently than he did others. John Morton, Archbishop, Cardinal, and Lord Chancellor, was a leading councillor both by virtue of his offices and because the king held him in high personal regard. Sir Reginald Bray, on the other hand, did not hold high office and his influence was entirely based upon confidence. The composition of the group which happened to be about the king at any given time was determined partly by Henry's express wish, and partly by accident. The distinction between regular and irregular councillors was perfectly well appreciated, but with a handful of exceptions it was not an *ex officio* distinction, and the idea that Henry VII's inner ring was the direct ancestor of Henry VIII's Privy Council can be abandoned.

Designation as a councillor did not necessarily imply that the king ever envisaged calling the person concerned to Council in the ordinary sense, and certainly not that he had some right of attendance without summons. The Council oath seems to have been administered only to those who attended upon a regular basis, and for the remainder the designation was largely honorific. It signified a special relationship with the king, far more so than a minor office at court, and a status which the bearer was expected to use in the king's service wherever he was normally resident. In other words a councillor was a trusted member of the king's affinity, and the title was sought after for that reason. For most of the peers who were so described, and whose usefulness to the king lay mainly within their own 'countries', it was an insurance against suspicion, and the debilitating effect which that could have upon their fortunes. They neither looked for nor received positions of responsibility within the central machinery of government. Henry's whole style of government was intensely personal. The most powerful men in England during Edward IV's reign had been either his kindred, like Richard of Gloucester, or favoured court peers like Lord Hastings. In 1497, however, well-informed Italian observers identified two prelates (Morton and Fox), one baron (Giles Daubeney) and two knights (Sir Reginald Bray and Sir Thomas Lovell) as the leading men of the realm. They also commented that the king's mother, Margaret Beaufort, was more influential than any minister or magnate;[6] an observation which no contemporary ever made about Elizabeth Woodville whatever Holinshed (or Shakespeare), who portrayed her as a powerful faction leader, may have said to the contrary. Henry's peers, both councillors and others, were well harnessed to the regime by 1509, but they were not pulling the main weight of the king's business. Their loyalty was more often assured by the negative process of entering into bonds and recognisances, which would be forfeited for unsatisfactory conduct, than by the positive ties of office and reward. These bonds sometimes carried penalties of several thousand pounds, and constituted powerful incentives to cooperation.

Henry VIII did not immediately change that situation. He discharged a number of burdensome recognisances, but he did not revolutionise the Council. Empson and Dudley became scapegoats to ease the passage of the old king's soul through purgatory, but Warham, Fox and Ruthal remained as key policy advisers. The eighteen-year-old Henry was already too shrewd to believe that he could do without the counsel of such wise heads. What he did do, and it did not meet with their approval at all, was to make bellicose noises about recovering his ancestors' rights in France. He probably did that more by instinct than by calculation, in search of a romantic and chivalric image to distinguish his reign from that of his calculating and somewhat arid father. However it also had the effect of rallying his peers behind him. Almost a generation had passed since the English nobility had seen serious action in the field, and many eager young men longed to emulate the deeds of their own forefathers. Relations between the old councillors and the king's military friends, such as the Earl of Surrey and Henry Courtenay, soon to become Earl of Devon, became increasingly strained. But it was not until war had actually broken out in 1512 that Henry found an adviser of his own who was able to take over the leadership of the Council. That man was Thomas Wolsey. Wolsey was a little over thirty in 1509, a generation younger than the men in power, but sufficiently senior to the king to impress him as a man of *gravitas* and experience. He had been at court as a royal chaplain since 1505, and had made himself useful in secondary diplomatic roles. He had obtained no office of significance, but he must have caught the attention of the young heir to the throne, because within a few months of his accession he made Wolsey his Almoner. This was hardly a major promotion, but it did involve a good deal of direct contact with the king, and the opportunity was not wasted. By 1511 his influence was already being commented upon, and it may well be that the ageing Fox saw Wolsey as his successor. It was, however, the military campaign of 1513 which really made the Almoner's fortune. He revealed himself to be a master of logistics, tireless in chivvying and harrying reluctant agents, and with an exemplary grasp of detail. Being a priest, he never went near a battlefield, and yet the capture of Tournai and the Battle of the Spurs owed more to his skill than to that of the soldiers. Not only that, but he was a kindred spirit of the ardent young king. When graver councillors urged their master to abandon his pastimes and devote his energies to affairs of state, Wolsey, with an eye to the main chance, urged the contrary.[7] This not only pleased Henry, it also enabled the Almoner to take on a far larger burden of work than would have been the case under a more diligent ruler, and to multiply the examples of his diligence and success. 'Who was now in high favour but Master Almoner? And who ruled all under the king but Master Almoner?', wrote Wolsey's gentleman usher George Cavendish many years later.[8]

This favour was quickly expressed in tangible terms. On 26 March 1514 he was consecrated Bishop of Lincoln, and in November of the same year translated to York on the death of Cardinal Bainbridge. Henry had already begun to press for his 'secret councillor' to be made a cardinal, and since Bainbridge had been the only English member of the College, the pope was sympathetic. The tangles of curial politics held up his elevation for about a year, but he was duly elected in August 1515. In December of the same year, following the resignation of William Warham, Wolsey also became Lord Chancellor, and thus the king's chief minister in name as well as in fact. For the next fifteen years he dominated the Council, and maintained such a high profile that some observers described him as *ipse rex* – the true king. We now know that that impression was highly deceptive, and that Henry was always in charge of his own realm. Nevertheless it was a contemporary view, and was not simply based upon the cardinal's lavish lifestyle. Wolsey himself never took his ascendency for granted. Although he did not spend much time at court, he tracked the king's movements assiduously, and seldom allowed more than a few days to elapse without personal contact.[9] His industry was astonishing, and one of the main foundations of his influence. Henry always listened to other advisers at his pleasure; Charles Brandon, the Duke of Suffolk and his brother-in-law, Sir William Compton, the Chief Gentleman of his Privy Chamber, and in the early days, Queen Catherine. Nevertheless the Lord Chancellor shouldered single-handed virtually the whole executive work of the Council. The formal Council continued to meet as it had done in Henry VII's reign, but its business declined in quantity and importance. At the same time the Council's equity jurisdiction became increasingly concentrated in special sessions which became known, rather misleadingly, as the court of Star Chamber. This designation gives the appearance of a distinct institution, but Star Chamber was not separate from the Council in any sense; nor was it a committee. Although some councillors specialised in Star Chamber business, all were entitled to sit, and many did so on an occasional basis. Wolsey worked hard at developing that aspect of the Council's work, partly because it was his proper concern as Chancellor and partly in order to give his fellow councillors something useful to do while he got on with the business of running the country.[10]

Wolsey virtually took over the functions of the old 'inner ring'. This had shown some signs of developing formality between 1509 and 1512, because Henry, for all his shrewdness and good sense, showed nothing like the appetite for work which his father had had, and his leading advisers had taken to meeting on their own initiative in order to keep up with the press of business. The new Lord Chancellor checked that development, and countermined the influence of the queen. Nevertheless his omnicompetence can easily be overestimated. When some of the mignons of the king's Privy Chamber overstepped the bounds of propriety in 1519, and 'played such light touches with him that they forgot themselves' they were removed and replaced by more sober gentlemen. It used to be thought that this was Wolsey's doing, and that the 'light touches' were a mere pretext for the dismissal of men whose rival influence he was beginning to fear. However it now seems clear that the cardinal had little or nothing to do with this episode, and that it was other senior councillors who persuaded Henry that his good nature was being abused.[11] Wolsey certainly conducted a feud with Sir William Compton, and eventually succeeded in dislodging him, but that was for a rather different reason. Similarly the resounding fall of the Duke of Buckingham in 1521 has been attributed to the cardinal's malice, but only the king himself could have decided to proceed to extremities against such a powerful subject. Wolsey may have encouraged Henry's suspicions, and used his own servants to collect evidence, but he did nothing to 'ensnare' the duke, who was largely the author of his own misfortune. At the same time the cardinal was an isolated figure. Of relatively humble origins, he was resented by the well-born councillors and courtiers who were compelled to defer to him, and lacked the support of any affinity or family network. He could find himself in the position of having responsibility without power. Having failed, partly through his own mismanagement, to obtain enough money from parliament in 1523 to meet the king's urgent needs, he was virtually constrained to suggest a forced loan or benevolence in 1525. The king accepted this advice with the consent of his whole Council, but when the project failed disastrously, it suddenly became Wolsey's exclusive responsibility. He had no option but to accept that situation, and endeavoured to divert popular anger away from his master by taking it upon himself.[12] However, instead of earning gratitude for such loyal service, he found that Henry had convinced himself of the truth of his *mea culpa* and that his whole position was compromised.

The Council might not exercise collective responsibility, but it could offer a certain collective security. Consequently, when the king began to express concern, later in 1525, that there never seemed to be any councillors around when he wanted them, Wolsey devised a scheme which seems to have been designed to restore the political and executive effectiveness of that body. The Council was to be reduced to twenty members, all of whom would be officers of state or household, who would discharge all existing responsibilities, including the judicial ones. This would have left the major part of the old Council to wither away, although whether it would have met the king's expressed concern may be doubted. When all contingencies had been taken into account, the councillors who were required to be 'in perpetual attendance' numbered only two. This would have left Wolsey free to deploy the majority at Westminster or elsewhere, as he had done over the past few years. Nevertheless had these Eltham Ordinances been implemented, the collective vitality of the more tightly organised Council might well have diminished the cardinal's authority. Perhaps for that reason, or perhaps because the king lost interest, they never were implemented during Wolsey's ascendancy, which lasted another three years.

The circumstances of his fall in 1529 are well-known, and do not need to concern us here, but the event itself restored the Council to the centre of the political stage. The Earl of Wiltshire, the Duke of Norfolk, the Duke of Suffolk and Sir Thomas More formed an inner ring in terms of their influence on the king, but they were a discordant group whose aims and policies diverged widely. Unaccustomed to orchestrating a divided Council, the king struggled to

find a sense of direction. He knew what he wanted to achieve, but
had no idea how to go about it. It was only with the emergence of
Thomas Cromwell as a significant influence in the Council towards
the end of 1532 that Henry's will began to drive a coherent policy.
Cromwell's influence over the next eight years was as great as that
of Wolsey had been, but his style was completely different. A self-
taught lawyer, his origins were even more humble than those of the
cardinal, but he avoided an ostentatious lifestyle and made no
attempt to turn his relatively modest household into a second court.
He seems to have cared little for the trappings of power, and
controlled the Council from a succession of second- and third-rank
offices before becoming Lord Privy Seal in 1536. Master of the
Jewel House in April 1532, he became Chancellor of the Exchequer
a year later, and Principal Secretary in the spring of 1534.
Although he was Secretary for only two years, he transformed that
office into the major clearing-house of administrative and political
business, a position which it retained even after he had moved on.
The manner of Cromwell's rise to power made him enemies, but he
was a far more dangerous man to cross than Wolsey had been, as
Thomas More, Anne Boleyn and the Marquis of Exeter all
discovered to their cost. He lived in a more dangerous world,
and for several years his own survival was closely tied to the success
of the revolutionary course upon which the king had embarked.
Unlike Wolsey, Cromwell made no attempt to elbow the Council
aside; his relationship with Henry required him to manage the
Council in the king's service, not take its place.[13]

This process reached a climax in the summer of 1536. The death
of Catherine in January and the execution of Anne in May had
raised expectations that the king's 'Great Matter' would be laid to
rest, and that its principal architect would fall from grace. Henry
brutally disillusioned such optimists, forcing the Princess Mary into
submission, and making it clear that he had no intention of
reopening negotiations with the papacy. One result of this was a
major rebellion in the north of England, known as the Pilgrimage
of Grace. Another was the reorganisation of the Council. No
recorded decision introduced this, but it closely followed the plan
laid down in the Eltham Ordinances of a decade earlier. Nineteen
named individuals, fifteen of whom held state or household offices,
constituted this new Council, which it is proper to describe as the
Privy Council. Whether these changes were the result of Crom-

well's initiative, of the king's belated recollection of his earlier intentions, or simply of pressing circumstances, is a matter of debate.[14] It was not entirely in Cromwell's interest to tighten the institutional structure of the Council in this manner, because it reduced his personal control of business, and may well have removed entirely any control which he exercised over attendance at meetings. On the other hand it reduced his exposure by increasing the credibility of the Council as an executive body, and that may well have been one of the main intentions. Just as the Amicable Grant had shaken Wolsey's credit with the king more than at first appeared, so the Pilgrimage of Grace did to Cromwell, and in the spring of 1540 he lost control of the Council which he had helped to create. Cromwell's fall in June 1540 and execution in July of that year ended Henry's dependence upon a single chief minister, and created a more corporate style of government. This was expressed on 10 August, when the Privy Council met to appoint a clerk and inaugerate a minute book. Council meetings had been minuted before, but only those formal sessions held during the law terms. That traditional practice was now abandoned, and the Privy Council met at all times of the year, when and where the king, or a president acting in the king's name, might determine. Thereafter meetings were held almost daily, and sometimes more than once a day, normally at court.

The king did not attend such sessions, which were mainly devoted to administrative and executive work. Warrants for payment were authorised, and letters of instruction sent out to local authorities. Delinquent officials and suspected criminals were summoned to attend and ordered to prison or bound in recognisances. A regular attendance of eight to ten members signified that many senior officials spent a large proportion of their working time attending Council meetings. When particularly sensitive issues were under discussion, or argument developed about what advice to give the king, the clerk was sent out of the room, so that the minutes, or 'Acts' reflect only the more mundane part of the ordinary business. Nevertheless the king did not normally take his advice from sessions of this sort, recorded or not, but from private sessions with individuals or with small groups of councillors. As before he listened to whom he pleased, and the emergence of the Privy Council made no difference to the decision-making process. Nor was the judicial work of Star Chamber much affected. The

Chief Justices of the two benches continued to sit there as 'councillors at large', despite the fact that they were not members of the
Privy Council. What did change was the level and focus of
administrative activity. Work which Wolsey had undertaken himself, and which Cromwell had tended to farm out among his own
servants, was now concentrated in an institution, the decisions of
which were recorded and could be followed up irrespective of the
comings and goings of individual councillors.

Even the smaller Privy Council after 1540 continued to be
politically and ideologically divided. Cranmer, Hertford and Paget
stood against Norfolk, Suffolk and Gardiner. Moreover the conservative ascendancy in the Council after Cromwell's fall was
balanced by a reforming ascendancy in the Privy Chamber. It
was the king's responsibility to resolve issues of that kind, and the
factional strife which divided the court between 1540 and 1547 did
not affect the Privy Council as an instrument of government.
However, the last months of Henry's life saw the rustication of
Stephen Gardiner, allegedly for a trivial misdemeanour over an
exchange of land, and the total fall of the Howards. The Duke of
Norfolk and his son were both convicted of high treason, and the
latter was executed in the last days of the king's life. As Suffolk had
died in 1545, the Paget/Hertford faction was unchallenged in
January 1547. This was not an accident, nor entirely the result of
their own successful intrigues. Henry had been personally and
deliberately responsible for both the destruction of Norfolk and
the exclusion of Gardiner.[15] The royal supremacy had been
Henry's masterpiece, and it had cost him dear. He was rightly
concerned over what would happen if his son succeeded as a minor,
and entrusted power to those whom he believed would be most
resistant to papal blandishments. Henry VIII's Privy Council
would, of course, be dissolved by his death, but by his will he
established a body of sixteen executors and twelve assistant executors, the majority of whom were Privy Councillors, who were
empowered to conduct the regency government in his son's name.
This was an eccentric and probably unworkable arrangement,
which may represent an incomplete intention, cut off by death,
or an implicit acknowledgement of the fact that the Earl of
Hertford and his allies would in any case shape a regime to suit
themselves. It is perhaps significant that Henry VIII never called a
Great Council. In each of the numerous crises of his reign it was the

parliament which was convened to give shape and force to the king's policies. After Henry VII's death the Great Council remained in abeyance until Charles I resorted to it on the eve of the Civil War, by which time nobody could remember how to conduct such an assembly, or what powers it was supposed to enjoy.

Within a few days of Henry's death, fourteen of his sixteen executors convened at the Tower of London to 'take order' for the regency government.[16] Predictably, they decided that power should be entrusted to a single person, and named the Earl of Hertford, the king's maternal uncle, as Lord Protector and Governor of the King's Person. However, they also stipulated that he should rule with the advice and consent of the Council, and promptly constituted themselves into the Privy Council of King Edward VI, actions which the nine-year-old boy was then called upon to endorse. In so far as there was a power struggle within the new Council, it came after these moves, and after the distribution of honours which followed them. On 16 February the new Lord Protector became Duke of Somerset, and Lord Chancellor Wriothesley became Earl of Southampton, promotions which, it was claimed, had been planned before Henry's death. However, within less than a month Wriothesley had been relieved of his office and dismissed from the Council, on what can only be described as a trivial pretext. It seems that his real offence was to object, not to the establishment of the Protectorate, but to the extension of the Protector's powers which was immediately proposed. On 12 March, with the consent, it appears, of the remainder of the Council, the restraints upon Somerset's authority were withdrawn by Letters Patent. He was then empowered to appoint new councillors at his pleasure, and no longer required to seek specific consent for all decisions of importance.[17] It soon transpired that this confidence, if such it was, was misplaced. In spite of a remarkable military success in Scotland in September 1547, by the spring of the following year the Protector was bogged down in a war which he need never have undertaken. His policy of controlling Scotland through garrisoned strongholds was proving expensive and unworkable. The French were poised to intervene, and he was no nearer achieving his object, which was a marriage between Edward and the infant Mary of Scotland. At home he had begun to move the English Church gently but unmistakably in a Protestant direction, demonstrating in the process that the royal supremacy was not personal to the king, but a part of the institutional authority of the English Crown. There was much discontent with this policy but little overt resistance. More seriously, his determined support for the moral crusade being launched against enclosure and the commercial exploitation of land by the so-called 'commonwealth men' was increasingly estranging him from the political nation. Aware that his support within the Council was crumbling, Somerset consulted it less and less. Research undertaken over twenty years ago demonstrated that the apparently smooth succession of well attended Council meetings was deceptive.[18] Sometimes the Council did not meet at all on the dates recorded; sometimes it met, but the attendance list was filled in later, and it is not known what relation it bore to the actual presence. The Protector made his own decisions, and often used his own household Council rather than the Privy Council to carry them out.

He was entitled to do that by the terms of his patent, but it was an extremely unwise course. Frustration, both over Scotland and over the enforcement of his social policy, made him short-tempered and autocratic. When he did meet the Council, he was brusque and ill-tempered. His friend and ally Sir William Paget became increasingly concerned:

> However it cometh to pass I cannot tell, but of late your grace is grown into great choleric fashions whensover you are contraried . . . Which . . . for God's sake consider and weigh well, and also when the whole Council shall move you, or give you advice in a matter (as they did of late for sending of men to Boulogne) to follow the same and to relent some time from your own opinion.[19]

Paget's advice was sensible and apposite, but the Protector had not been listening for some time. Instead he increasingly lost touch with reality. A French army landed in Scotland in the summer of 1548, and the Scots immediately signed the treaty of Haddington, committing their young queen to a marriage with the dauphin. In August she departed for France, and the whole foundation of Somerset's Scottish policy was destroyed. At the same time he assiduously ignored the warning signs that his social policy was stirring up serious trouble. As the enclosure commissioners began their operations in the summer of 1548, riots broke out in their wake, and Somerset's fellow councillor and erstwhile ally the Earl of Warwick was not slow to point out the connection.[20] The Protector paid no heed. In January 1549 he got his important and controversial bill for religious uniformity through parliament, and appears to have believed that his position was unassailable.

The autumn of 1549 brought dramatic disillusionment. Undeterred by the experiences of the previous year, Somerset had resumed the enclosure commissions in the early summer, and by mid-July there were major disorders across the whole of central and southern England. As the Council struggled to contain the situation, the Protector's attitude appeared to be ambivalent. He was reluctant to respond swiftly, or with sufficient force. This was partly because he refused until the very last moment to abandon a projected campaign to restablish the English position in Scotland, and thus release sufficient troops to put down the risings. It was also because he saw the justice of some, at least, of the rebels' complaints. However, the head of a government so comprehensively threatened could not afford to be scrupulous. In three areas, Oxfordshire, Norfolk and the south-west, the situation was for a few weeks out of control. Eventually the risings were suppressed by force at the cost of many lives, but the Protector did not take the field in person. Consequently Lord Grey, Lord Russell and the Earl of Warwick got the credit for the victories which were won in the field, and Somerset's position became weaker rather than stronger. In the midst of these troubles, and obviously seeking to take advantage of them, in early August the king of France declared war with the objective of recovering Boulogne, lost to Henry VIII six years earlier. By early September the Council had returned to life, inspired by a common sense of purpose. The Protector must go.

On 10 October, after a series of carefully planned moves by sixteen or seventeen members of the Privy Council who had gathered in London for the purpose, Somerset was overthrown. His offices were left vacant, and eventually abolished. At first it appeared that the consensus which had been created to remove the Protector would endure, and that the regency government, which still had some six years to run, would return to the collective format apparently envisaged in the late king's will. That did not happen because the Council was divided on the important issue of religion. Many expected the end of the Protectorate to signal the end of

Protestant advance, and a return to the settlement of 1543. However Archbishop Cranmer remained committed to the changes which had been made, and the Earl of Warwick shrewdly perceived that the young king's own developing convictions were more than a mere adolescent fancy. Anyone who wished to retain Edward's favour after 1555 would be well-advised to pay attention to his present wishes. By Christmas the earl had outmanoeuvred his conservative opponents and secured control of the Council.[21] The Earl of Arundel and several of his supporters were removed from the board, and replaced by Protestants such as the Bishop of Ely and the Marquis of Dorset. Warwick became Lord President, but he made no attempt to imitate Somerset's style of rule, and the Council entered a new and important phase of its life. Sir William Paget, who had been raised to the peerage in November 1549, was no great friend of Warwick's, but he did know how to organise the Council's business, and under his guidance it soon returned to orderly and purposeful ways. At some point during 1550 he drew up a memorandum of guidance, which seems to have been broadly followed.[22] This started with pious exhortations about the need for brotherly love, but soon descended to the practical:

> Item, that six at least of the Privy Council be continually attendant in the court, whereof the lord chancellor or lord treasurer or lord great master or lord chamberlain to be two and one of the secretaries to be a third, and that the six in the absence of the rest may pass the affairs current, and shall have their proceedings ratified by the rest when they come.

The memorandum then went on to spell out in some detail the daily and weekly routines to be followed, and the proper method of keeping the register. This was very much the working Council of officeholders which Cromwell had envisaged, but with one important difference. It was actually responsible for making the decisions upon which it acted, as distinct from executing the will of an adult king. On at least two occasions Edward himself drew up papers connected with the organisation and discharge of Council business, which certainly demonstrates his interest in the subject.[23] They do not, however, prove that he was beginning to assume control before the onset of his final illness. If his memoranda were intended to be prescriptive, no one paid much attention to them, and it seems more reasonable to assume that they were exercises produced by the rapidly maturing king as a part of the practical education in politics and administration to which he was being subjected by the Earl of Warwick.

Given the high level of social tension which persisted after 1549, and the continuing implementation of unpopular religious reforms, the effectiveness of the Council in the latter part of Edward's reign was remarkable. Police work took up a great deal of time. Reports were received from justices of the peace and other local officials. Investigations were set up, and sometimes arrests were ordered. Warwick was generally disliked and suspected by ordinary people partly because of his tough line over civil disorder, and partly because of his responsibility for the eventual execution of the Duke of Somerset in January 1552. However, in a sense this was an advantage to him. Thoroughly alarmed by the widespread and recent disaffection, of which they had been the principal targets, the gentry and aristocracy realised that they had to appear united in support of the Council. By the same token the Council itself could not afford factions or internal disputes. It was because of his incorrigible opposition to Warwick and his unwillingness to play as a member of the team that the fallen Protector had eventually to be removed. Fear, or at least nervousness, therefore made Warwick's regime appear a good deal more solid than it really was. Religious conservatives accepted the Prayer Book of 1552 and the commission on Church goods, both of which they intensely disliked, in preference to causing trouble which might have been seized upon by popular agitators. Warwick also used the Council wisely. He consulted them and involved them in every aspect of executive and administrative work. Government debts were reduced, and the reorganisation of the revenue courts was ordered. Peace was kept abroad, but money was spent upon the upkeep of the navy, and in Ireland.[24] Warwick adjusted the membership of the Council to suit himself. An early purge of conservative opponents was followed by the steady recruitment of his own friends and supporters – William Cecil, Sir John Gates, Lord Clinton and others. Paget was finally dropped at the time of Somerset's fall, and his reliable friend the Marquis of Dorset was promoted to be Duke of Suffolk. Meanwhile the king was acclimatised. Special Council meetings were staged for his benefit and in his presence. William Thomas, one of the Council clerks, was prompted to feed him position papers and to encourage him to try out his ideas upon his advisers.[25] How much difference Edward's participation made to the Council may be doubted, but it certainly made a difference to him. He became more confident, and perhaps began to believe that he was already assuming control. His relationship with the Earl of Warwick became, and remained, excellent.

As a strategy designed to keep Warwick (Duke of Northumberland from November 1551) and his friends in power, this was extremely well-conceived, and it did no harm to the government. Had Edward lived, Northumberland might well have been remembered as one of the most successful politicians of the century. But Edward did not live, and Northumberland's attempt to preserve the consensus by which he had ruled beyond the king's life was a disastrous failure. The reasons for this were numerous, and cannot be explored in this context, but the basic fact was that when Edward began to think about the succession in January 1553, he came to the implacable decision that his half-sister Mary, the heir by his father's last Succession Act, was unacceptable. What argument or persuasion may have taken place we do not know, but by the time that the king's illness was known to be mortal, early in June 1553, he and Northumberland were agreed that the Succession Act must be set aside, and the Crown settled on Jane Grey, the eldest daughter of the Duke of Suffolk and a granddaughter of Henry VIII's younger sister, Mary. It was a quixotic and illogical decision, and many councillors were appalled when it was revealed to them. However, there could be no question of refusing the king's express command, sick though he was, and it scarcely needed Northumberland's dominant personality to establish an ostensible agreement to accept the new succession. On 6 July Edward died, and Jane was duly proclaimed. However, Mary immediately counter-claimed, and for about a week the issue hung in the balance. Then the Council split, the lead being taken by some of those whom Northumberland had brought back in an attempt to broaden the consensus of support for Jane, notably Lord Paget and the Earl of Arundel.[26] Once the spell of Northumberland's ascendancy was broken, his position collapsed in a few days, and Mary was proclaimed in London on 19 of July. Whatever apprehensions may have existed about how the new Queen would use her power, or how others might use her, the lawful order had been upheld, and England embarked upon the unprecedented experiment of a female ruler.

Because of the controversial circumstances of her accession, and because of her detachment from the main events of English politics over the previous six years, the construction of Mary's Privy Council presented many difficulties. As self-styled queen she needed a Council at once, but the only men available on 10 July were the household officers already in her service. Consequently Mary had to construct her initial Council out of very unpromising material, and the so-called 'Framlingham councillors' were to remain as a distinct and sometimes difficult group within the full Council throughout the short reign. It was only when the London Council split, and the major part declared for her, that Mary could begin to command the services of experienced men. She was then faced with the great difficulty of how to respond to the submission of men who only days before had been denouncing her as a pretender, but without whose assistance she could hardly hope to govern. The position which she adopted was sensible and pragmatic. Early arrivals like Arundel and Paget, who had only slight connections with Northumberland, were welcomed and immediately employed. Magnates such as the Earls of Shrewsbury and Pembroke were welcomed more cautiously. Some, including the Lord Treasurer, were kept for days or weeks in limbo before being rehabilitated; others were placed under house arrest.[27] Finally the core of the Dudley faction – the duke himself, his sons, the Duke of Suffolk and the Marquis of Northampton – were consigned to the Tower or other suitable prisons.

By the time that Mary had finished building her Council at the end of August, it numbered over forty, and was a very hetero-geneous body. In addition to the Framlingham group and the former Edwardian councillors, who eyed each other with mutual suspicion and dislike, there were also those former councillors of her father who had fallen out of favour and were languishing in prison – the Duke of Norfolk, Cuthbert Tunstall, Bishop of Durham, and Stephen Gardiner, Bishop of Winchester. Of these only Gardiner still had the energy to be an active councillor, but as Lord Chancellor he immediately became one of the queen's leading advisers. As a source of political advice and support to the monarch, this Council never worked.[28] That was not the result of its size. The number of regular attenders was no greater than in the previous reign, and many of those who were styled councillors were employed most of the time at a distance from the court. The responsibility for this malfunctioning rested entirely with the queen. Because of her inexperience she expected her councillors to give her unanimous advice, and when they quarrelled and disagreed, as councillors always did, she became distressed and suspicious of their loyalty. Gardiner and Paget were old enemies, and disagreed on a wide range of issues, but neither of them would have dreamed of conspiring against their mistress, and she was less than just to each of them in turn. Part of the problem was that, apart from the Framlingham group, virtually all Mary's councillors had at one time or another supported and implemented policies of which she strongly disapproved. Instead of following her grandfather's practice, and putting away the past, she employed them, but never entirely trusted them no matter how devoted they proved. This not only promoted factiousness, it also encouraged her to look outside the Council for crucial advice. In the first year of her reign this was supplied by the Imperial ambassador, Simon Renard, in the second by her husband, Philip of Spain, and thereafter by her kinsman Cardinal Reginald Pole.[29]

The consequences of this were serious. In the spring of 1554 she allowed the Lord Chancellor to propose legislation for her second parliament without briefing his colleagues in advance, with the result that Lord Paget successfully opposed his bill in the House of Lords, and attracted the queen's extreme anger in consequence. In spite of speaking no English, and being unfamiliar with English practices, Philip had a surer touch with the Privy Council than Mary had. When he left England in August 1555, he set up a 'select council' to keep him in touch with English affairs, although whether that ever had any distinct identity outside the king's mind may be a matter of doubt. The Council was properly consulted over the decision to go to war with France in 1557, and its uniquely unanimous advice was ignored. On one occasion Mary complained that she spent all her time shouting at her Council, but to no avail. If that was true, it was a comment on the queen rather than the Council, but we must also remember that much of the evidence for this uneasy relationship comes from Imperial sources and is not, therefore, objective or disinterested. Both Renard and the Count of Feria, Philip's representative in England, sought to justify their interference in English affairs by pleading the incompetence of the Council, but 'incompetence' should be glossed as an unwillingness to fulfil their wishes. Renard in particular was repeatedly eloquent on the subject of the quarrels and confusions within the English Council, and urged the queen to reduce it in size. Several times he believed that he was on the verge of success, but in fact Mary had neither the will nor the need to pursue such a policy.

Whatever the Imperial diplomats may have thought, there were many advantages in a large Council. In a sense Mary restored a representative aspect, because she recruited men of several different backgrounds and points of view. More importantly, a large Council could be divided into a number of different groups and working parties for special purposes. These were not committees in the proper sense, because they did not report back, but in February 1554 no fewer than twelve groups were set up for a variety of purposes from calling in debts to preparing legislation for parliament.[30] One group was to remain permanently in London. The others presumably met wherever and whenever convenience served, while the main body of the Council followed the court. This method of working also seems to have been followed on other occasions, with considerable success. Mary's Council, like Edward's, concerned itself much with police work and, rather more surprisingly, with the enforcement of religious uniformity. The restoration of papal jurisdiction did not remove spiritual matters entirely from the temporal sphere. In theory the Council was supporting the Cardinal Legate and the episcopate, but in practice a strong flavour of the royal supremacy lingered. The manager of Council business during this reign, except for his months of disfavour in the summer of 1554, was Lord Paget – Lord Privy Seal from 1555 – who had been trained in the Cromwellian school of administration. It is possible that working parties may have encouraged divisions and misunderstandings among councillors, but most evidence suggests that in its executive and administrative capacities, the Marian Council functioned efficiently, and that the country was being effectively governed when Mary died in November 1558. Whatever political failures and frustrations the queen may have endured, there was no breakdown of civil order, and the control which her Council exercised was probably superior to that of her predecessor.

The principal beneficiary of this success was Elizabeth, who was undistracted by opposition or civil disorder at the time of her succession. To what extent she had already assembled a shadow Council during the last weeks of Mary's life is uncertain, but the rapid advance of that group of university-trained gentlemen, known from their intellectual tastes as the 'Athenians', in both court and Council at the end of 1558, indicates a measure of forethought and preparation. The new queen immediately abandoned the expanded format which had been forced upon her predecessor, returning the Privy Council to its Cromwellian size of twenty. Less than a quarter of Mary's councillors retained their seats, but they formed exactly half the new Council. The most distinguished survivor was the Lord Treasurer, the Marquis of Winchester, who had similarly survived the fall of the Duke of Northumberland. Gardiner had died in 1555, and Cardinal Pole on the same day as his mistress, but Paget was discarded, his vast experience not outweighing his close association with Philip. Sir William Cecil returned to the office of Principal Secretary, which he had also held under Edward VI, and quickly became the key man in the new administration. In most respects Elizabeth's choice of councillors was orthodox. Old Henricians like Winchester, Shrewsbury and Arundel were balanced against Edwardian Protestants such as Cecil, Bacon and Bedford. Most also had experience of senior office. The only unusual feature was the absence of prelates. Nicholas Wotton was technically in orders, but for the first time since the Tudors gained the throne no bishop sat on Elizabeth's Privy Council. It was not until 1583 that John Whitgift assumed the position which had always been regarded as belonging to the Archbishop of Canterbury *ex officio*. One other significant name was missing from the early Council. It was not until 1562 that Lord Robert Dudley was sworn. Before that the queen's favourite and putative lover was a rogue element on the political scene. His appointment to the Council probably coincided with Elizabeth's acceptance of the political impossibility of marrying him, and represented his 'normalisation' as a royal adviser.

Elizabeth's Privy Council remained the focus of her government, but the records, almost complete from 1540 to 1558, show substantial gaps in both the 1560s and the 1580s. This is not on account of any change of secretarial practice, or any deficiency in record-keeping, but rather of the chances of survival. It was by no means uncommon for ministers to treat state papers as their own personal property. The Cecil archive at Hatfield provides an excellent example of the consequences, and it is quite possible that several Elizabethan Council books fell into the hands of officers less fortunate in their posterity. It is possible, but not likely, that this may have caused some significant development of conciliar practice or procedure to pass unnoticed. However it seems clear that, as an institution, Elizabeth's Council had little political history of its own, and in that it presents a marked contrast to the Councils of her two predecessors. Councillors disagreed fiercely about ways and means, but not about ends. Such issues as the fate of Mary Queen of Scots, or the extent of the English commitment in the Low Countries, provoked raging disputes and caused parties to form in the court, but the Council itself remained too small and compact to become divided by faction. Dwindling slowly but steadily in size, by 1601 it numbered only thirteen members. This did not reflect a loss of power, rather the contrary, but it did signify a much more unified method of operation than had prevailed in the 1550s. There were no special groups, standing or *ad hoc*, with the exception of the court of Star Chamber, which was virtually a separate institution by the end of the century, and consequently no footholds for factional activity to develop.

Elizabeth was not particularly adroit at handling quarrels among her councillors. Both the disagreement between Robert Dudley and William Cecil in the 1560s and that between the Earl of Essex and Robert Cecil in the 1590s were unnecessarily protracted and acrimonious because of her hesitancy and unwillingness to make clear decisions.[31] Both were personal in origin, but involved policy issues of some importance. The queen made, or did not make, her own decisions, and throughout her long reign the business of providing political advice remained in the hands of individual councillors or *ad hoc* groups. It was never a function of the Council as a whole. Elizabeth neither expected nor welcomed unanimous advice, and was very disconcerted when she received it, especially if it did not correspond with her wishes. That was one of the reasons why the unfortunate William Davidson became the scapegoat for the execution of Mary Queen of Scots, and why councillors were so often forced to resort to underhand tactics in parliament in order to put pressure upon her. By the 1590s the main function of the Privy Council was to control the workings of local government, particularly the Lords Lieutenant and the great variety of commissions. It issued proclamations in the queen's name and supervised the enforcement of administrative statutes. The Ordnance Office, the Admiralty, and the courts of Star Chamber and High Commission were all responsible for their own specialist functions, and the Privy Council was beginning to resemble the later Home Office. In theory nothing had changed, but in practice the functions of this central institution of government had become both more focused and more bureaucratic.

Notes

1. R. Virgoe, 'The composition of the king's Council, 1437–61', *Bulletin of the Institute of Historical Research*, 43 (1970) pp. 134–60.
2. C. L. Scofield, *The Life and Reign of Edward IV*, vol. I (1923) pp. 376–8; J. R. Lander, 'Council, Administration and Councillors, 1461–1485', *BIHR*, 32 (1959); C. Ross, *Edward IV* (1974) p. 311 and n.
3. S. B. Chrimes, *Henry VII* (1972) pp. 100–2.
4. R. Somerville, 'Henry VII's "Council Learned in the Law"', *English Historical Review*, 54 (1939) pp. 427–42; Chrimes, *Henry VII*, p. 99 and n.
5. Chrimes, *Henry VII*, pp. 98–9.
6. R. Brown (ed.), *Calendar of State Papers, Venetian*, vol. I (1864) p. 256; *Calendar of State Papers, Spanish*, vol. I, and *Supplements*, G. A. Bergenroth (ed.), (1862, 1868) p. 163 and supplement p. 131; *Select Cases in the Council of Henry VII*, C. G. Bayne and W. H. Dunham (eds) (Selden Society, (1964) pp. xl, xli.
7. George Cavendish, *The Life and Death of Cardinal Wolsey*, ed. R. S. Sylvester (Early English Text Society, (1959) p. 13.
8. Ibid.
9. N. Samman, 'The Tudor Court during the ascendency of Cardinal Wolsey' (1989) Ph.D thesis, University of Wales, Appendix.
10. J. A. Guy, *The Cardinal's Court: The Impact of Thomas Wolsey on Star Chamber* (Brighton, 1977).
11. Hall's *Chronicle* (1809) p. 598; D. Starkey, 'Intimacy and Innovation: the rise of the Privy Chamber, 1485–1547', in *The English Court from the Wars of the Roses to the Civil War* (1987); D. Loades, *The Tudor Court* (1992) p. 48.
12. G. W. Bernard, *War, Taxation and Rebellion in Early Tudor England: Henry VIII, Wolsey and the Amicable Grant of 1525* (Brighton, 1986)
13. J. A. Guy, 'The Privy Council: Revolution or Evolution?' in D. Starkey and C. Coleman (eds), *Revolution Reassessed* (1986) pp. 67–8; A. Fox and J. A. Guy, *Reassessing the Henrician Age* (1986) pp. 135–6.
14. *Reassessing the Henrician Age*, pp. 135–6. See also G. R. Elton, *The Tudor Revolution in Government* (1953) pp. 316–52.
15. J. Scarisbrick, *Henry VIII* (1968) pp. 482–3; Glyn Redworth, *In Defence of the Church Catholic: The Life of Stephen Gardiner* (1990) pp. 244–6.
16. J. R. Dasent *et al.* (eds) *Acts of the Privy Council* (1890–1964) vol. II, pp. 3–4.
17. *Calendar of the Patent Rolls, Edward VI*, vol. I, p. 97.

18. D. E. Hoak, *The King's Council in the Reign of Edward VI* (Cambridge, 1976).
19. Public Record Office, SP10/8 no. 4.
20. J. Strype, *Ecclesiastical Memorials* (1822) vol. II, pt. ii, pp. 149–52.
21. H. James, 'The aftermath of the 1549 coup, and the Earl of Warwick's intentions', *Historical Research*, 62 (1989); D. Loades, *Essays on the Reign of Edward VI* (1994) pp. 80–6.
22. British Library, Egerton MS 2603, ff. 33–4.
23. W. K. Jordan, *The Chronicle and Political Papers of Edward VI* (1966) pp. 176–83.
24. S. G. Ellis, *Tudor Ireland: Crown, Community and the Conflict of Cultures, 1470–1603* (1985) pp. 229–30; D. Loades, *The Tudor Navy* (1992) pp. 152–5.
25. British Library, Cotton MS Vespasian D xviii, ff. 2–45; E. R. Adair, 'William Thomas', in R.W. Seton Watson (ed.), *Tudor Studies* (1924) pp. 133–8.
26. E. H. Harbison, *Rival Ambassadors at the Court of Queen Mary* (Princeton, 1940) pp. 49–50.
27. D. Loades, *The Reign of Queen Mary* (1991) pp. 20–4.
28. Ibid., pp. 193–231.
29. Ibid., pp. 194–5.
30. Dasent *et al.* (eds) *Acts of the Privy Council*, vol. IV, pp. 397–9.
31. J. A. Guy, *Tudor England* (1988) pp. 439–40; L. B. Smith, *Treason in Tudor England* (1986) pp. 218–38.

4   The Royal Commissions

Commissions were Letters Patent, issued over the Great Seal of England and authorising named individuals to carry out certain functions on the king's behalf. Some, like the revenue commission of 1552, established enquiries where the commissioners' instructions were to investigate a specific situation and to make recommendations for action.[1] A similar group was set up in 1549 to draft a new code of canon law for the reformed English Church. Such commissions were time-limited, and the eventual outcome of their labours was not under their own control. They might report personally to the monarch, or to the Lord Chancellor, but more commonly to the Council. The revenue commission reported in December 1552, but some of its conclusions were suppressed before they ever reached the Council. Those which were presented were accepted, but very patchily implemented.[2] The report of the canon law commission was rejected outright in March 1553, and the commission expired with the end of Edward's last parliament. When such groups were dealing with important public issues, they were composed of senior officials and Privy Councillors, but a commission of enquiry for a local purpose would be made up of suitably qualified local men. After 1570, for example, most counties had commissions to investigate the incidence of recusancy. It was not the function of such groups to try or punish offending Catholics, but to bring their activities to light and make sure that they were referred to the appropriate court. Similarly the enclosure commissions established by the Lord Protector in 1548 were given a long list of questions to ask on a parish-by-parish basis, but they had no powers to act against those who were denounced, even where a clear infringement of the law was indicated. This inevitably caused frustration, especially since the instructions also included an explicit warning that no one was to take the law into their own hands on the basis of what was discovered.[3]

A second type of commission was administrative. Direct taxation was assessed by such means, and often also collected. Commissions conducted county musters, until they were superseded in that function by the deputy lieutenants. Commissioners compounded for purveyance, when it was eventually decided that the quota system which had been devised to make the random depredations of household and naval officers more equitable was no longer working. And the delightfully named commissions of sewers were responsible for surveying dykes, waterways and drainage systems in order to identify necessary repairs. Unlike commissions of enquiry, which had power only to call witnesses to give evidence before them, these administrative commissions did have some coercive force. Muster commissioners could punish defaulters, and commissioners of sewers could order the necessary repair work to be done. However it was the judicial commissions which really carried the weight of the king's authority. These empowered their bearers in various ways to administer the common law in the king's name, and to inflict the full range of penalties available to the courts at Westminster. Judicial commissions took three main forms; gaol delivery, the peace, and oyer and terminer. The last was the most flexible, but also the most straightforward. Its limits were internally defined, in so far as it gave its bearers authority to hear all pleas of the Crown within a given area, and for a given period of time. There were such things as standing commissions of oyer and terminer, to which we will be returning in due course, but the great majority were occasional in nature. This was the commission which was borne by the Assize judges on their circuits, and it was regularly used for the trial of treason or piracy, where exceptional expedition was required or the defendants were particularly numerous. All judicial commissions were used to bring the royal authority directly to bear upon wrongdoers, but oyer and terminer was the most explicit. It was unusual for such commissioners to be local men, and local influences were rigourously excluded from the process of nomination. Assize judges, for example, were senior professional lawyers, often drawn from outside the circuit which they were called upon to ride, and commissions dealing with piracy were headed by the Lord Admiral and the Admiralty judge. The Tudors did not invent this type of commission. Its roots were ancient and it had been used extensively by Edward IV, but they made it peculiarly their own, and it remained an exceptionally effective way of bringing the central authority of the Crown to bear upon all parts of the kingdom.

Gaol delivery, as its name suggests, was a single-purpose commission. Such justices were named as required, usually when a backlog of cases had caused the prison in a particular place to be overfull. Their powers were the same as those of justices of the peace. They were not required to be legally trained, and they were expected to refer cases presenting technical difficulties to the assizes. It would be an exaggeration to say that they dealt only with minor matters, because some of the cases which they heard carried the death penalty, but by the sixteenth century they had become supplementary to the assize circuits. By far the most important of the judicial commissions in the Tudor period was the commission of the peace. This had originated in the fourteenth century as a supplement to the existing provision of assizes, county and hundred courts. It was probably intended from the beginning to broaden the basis of royal government in the counties by involving a larger number of local gentlemen, and that was certainly its effect. The qualification for selection was 'substance', and that did not simply mean wealth, but also honour and respect in the community. The function of these justices was originally confined to enforcing the statutes of the peace, to receiving indictments which covered most pleas of the Crown, and to conducting trials by jury. They discharged these duties in judicial sessions held four times a year, and known for that reason as quarter sessions. At first these commissioners had numbered no more than four or five per county, but that had increased to about a dozen before the end of Edward IV's reign. Theoretically the commission was renewed annually, although practice had varied somewhat from one reign to another.

It was Henry VII who began to transform this limited instrument into a powerful and flexible agency of government by adding administrative to judicial responsibilities, and by commissioning one or more councillors in every county. By the time that Sir Thomas Smith described its nature in 1565, the commission of the peace had expanded to thirty or forty members per county, headed in every case by 'high nobility and chief magistrates for honour's sake'.[4] Smith attributed the increase in scale both to an increase in the numbers and wealth of the gentry, and to a better will to serve. The presence of nobles and 'chief magistrates' was not purely honorific, although they hardly ever attended to the normal work of a justice. Their function was to use their prestige and their court connections to prevent their colleagues from stepping out of line on issues where local feelings might differ from official policy. The expansion of these commissions, and the diversification of their work, necessitated a certain amount of professional stiffening, and the quorum was introduced. This consisted of a small core group of professionally trained lawyers, who were also ideally gentlemen of the county, one or two of whom had always to be present when decisions of importance were being taken. The purpose of this was not only to prevent embarrassing mistakes, but also to reduce the number of cases which required referral to the assizes. The appointment of a professionally trained Clerk of the Peace represented a further step in the same direction, as did the creation of the office of *Custos Rotulorum*. The *Custos* was a senior and respected justice, who was not only responsible for keeping the records, but who also presided at the quarter sessions and was the functional head of the commission.

The method of appointing justices of the peace was in theory simple, but in practice often a complex game of political manoeuvring. By the middle of Henry VIII's reign, and probably for some time before that, service on the commission was prestigious. This was reflected in Smith's identification of a better will to serve as one of the reasons for the increase in the size of the commissions. So much was this so that by the early part of Elizabeth's reign the status of justice of the peace was fiercely competed for by the middling gentry of every county. In every shire there was a handful of major families whose wealth and general respect ensured that the head was always a justice, and sometimes his eldest son in his lifetime. Below that level, the patronage of peers and councillors, court connections, and the outcomes of local feuds, could all be important. In the late 1590s bad blood between the Lovell and Gawdy families in Norfolk inspired Bassingbourne Gawdy to accuse his rival of inciting his neighbours to refuse contributions towards the arming of the county levies. Sir Thomas Lovell had left himself open to such a charge, and he was summoned before the Council as 'an evill example to the inferior sort which are backward inough to pay unto such charges'. He was dismissed from the commission of the peace, and imprisoned in the Marshalsea.[5] Such drastic action was probably uncommon, but suspicion recusancy, even if not substantiated, could be fatal to an aspirant, and proven recusancy debarred even the most substantial, especially after 1580. The Lord Chancellor nominated the commissioners, but his choice was guided by those whom he chose to consult, or who were able to gain his ear. A Privy Councillor resident in the county was a natural contact, but the judges who rode the assize circuits provided better coverage. The role of major peers in this connection changed as the century advanced. In the 1520s no one would have gainsaid the choice of the Marquis of Exeter or the Earl of Northumberland in their 'countries', although the Chancellor would have insisted upon naming the leading members of the king's affinity as well. The fall of these great families, however, left something of a political vacuum which new peerage families such as the Dudleys and the Russells were unable to fill. As late as the 1560s the Duke of Norfolk was deferred to in respect of appointments in East Anglia, but after his execution there was no single ascendant family or individual, and the gentry families fell into competing groups or factions.[6] Powerful Elizabethan peers like the Earl of Leicester and the Earl of Essex had widespread influence, but they were both court-based and controversial, lacking the automatic deference accorded to some of their predecessors.

The reasons why service as a justice of the peace was so much sought after are clear enough. Nomination was a sign of royal favour or confidence. A justice of the peace was the king's man, to the extent that he was not permitted to wear the livery of any other lord. As the range of his activities increased, he became the most familiar and easily recognisable representative of royal authority. The justice licensed alehouses, fixed wage rates and sometimes prices in accordance with statutes for that purpose, and investigated every complaint of crime or misdemeanour. One member of the quorum, sitting with one or two others, could hold special sessions of the peace at his discretion. These might be for a specific purpose, or they might be to deal with a range of minor misdemeanours which could be handled summarily. For this reason they were later known as the petty sessions. This ubiquitous jurisdiction not only gave the justice an unrivalled knowledge of the community for which he was responsible, it also gave him the power which that knowledge conferred. How was an ordinary man to know when a gentleman was speaking as a justice, and when in his private capacity as a landlord or employer? In 1554 a Dorset gentleman, troubled with fractious tenants, reported in his capacity as a JP that they were in rebellion against the Queen's authority. News of this alleged rebellion spread panic across the south of England until the Council discovered the truth and consigned the offending magistrate to prison. Justices were, or could be, paid their expenses for attending quarter sessions, but in other respects their work was unpaid. It was not, however, unrewarded. In every county there were scores of minor offices and sinecures in the monarch's gift: keeperships of royal parks and chases, stewardships of demesne manors, constableships of minor or decayed castles, and many others.[7] It was understood that local gentlemen had the first claim upon such morsels, and the justices were in the best position to benefit. A few were remunerative in themselves; others created opportunities for profit, such as the aulnagers who affixed the required quality seals to every bale of cloth; other were desirable because they were of 'estimacion in the country', irrespective of financial gain. By the reign of Elizabeth the gentry of every shire were bound to the Crown by a steadily thickening web of such preferments. Their social dominance was recognised and rein-forced, and in return they governed the country in the queen's name.

The importance of this mutuality was clearly recognised at the time. Sir Thomas Smith waxed eloquent with enthusiasm:

> The justices of the peace do meet also at other times by commandment of the prince upon suspicion of war, or to take order for the safety of the shire, sometimes to take musters of harness and able men, and sometimes to take order for the excessive wages of labourers and servants, for excess of apparel, for unlawful games, for conventicles and evil orders in ale houses and taverns, for punishment of idle and vagabond persons, and generally, as I have said, for the good government of the shire the prince putteth his confidence in them.[8]

William Lambarde clearly thought the same. Nearly twenty years later, in 1587, he wrote a comprehensive guide to the duties of a justice of the peace, entitled *Eirenarcha*, which enables us to reconstruct every aspect of the commission's work. He also kept a diary, unpublished in his own lifetime, which reflects his experiences as a JP in Kent. He records that he was named to the commission on 6 August 1579, and took the oath of office on 3 June following. Thereafter

> The last of June 1580 and the first of July I joined with my father-in-law, George Moulton, in the examination of Baptiste

Bristow, Edward Rootes, John Romyne, Thomas Missenden and Nicholas Miller concerning a robbery done upon the said Baptiste etc. by virtue of letters received from the lords of the Privy Council.[9]

Week by week he noted action taken in fulfilment of Council instructions. On 26 August he was at Tonbridge 'in the execution of the commission of sewers for Medway'. There he committed to prison several unlicensed alehouse-keepers, which, along with the taking of recognisances, was his most frequent judicial action. At the end of September he certified to the bishop that one Margaret Trebold was of good behaviour. She was about to be married, and it is probable that her intended husband was a clergyman, whose spouses had to be vetted in this way, both by the bishop and by two justices of the peace. From the pages of this diary we get a vivid impression of a group of gentlemen who knew each other well, and who were married into each other's families, controlling many aspects of the daily lives of their poorer neighbours as well as enforcing the law in the ordinary sense. In a society without a professional police force, the habitual obedience and deference which were accorded to the justices were the best guarantee of public order. The main reason why the disturbances of 1548 and 1549 had appeared to be so threatening had been precisely that they had challenged that subordination. When the Earl of Warwick feared that he could not command the loyalty of his own men, and when Kett's followers were declaring that 'there were too many gentlemen in England by 500', the Council felt that it was staring into the abyss.[10]

Order was restored by force, but for a decade after 1549 the gentry of southern and eastern England went in fear of another 'camping summer'. That did not happen, but the crisis had drawn attention to two circumstances which needed to be borne in mind. In the first place there were justices who abused their powers, and whose activities were not only detrimental to the sovereign's honour, but a threat to the order they were supposed to be protecting. And secondly it was useless for the Council, or the monarch, to issue orders, in whatever form, which the justices were not prepared to enforce. The Protector's social policy had been high-minded, and strictly in accordance with tradition, but it had been directly contrary to the interests of the gentry as landlords and employers. A more pragmatic approach was essential, and was successfully adopted for the remainder of the century. The discipline of the justices themselves was in the hands of the Council, and the Council could only act upon information received, so a system of notifying actionable misdemeanours was required. At first Henry VII was so short of usable alternatives that he had to order the commissioners to invite criticisms of themselves. A statute of 1489 required that a proclamation should be read at every quarter sessions, instructing the justices collectively to receive and act upon complaints directed against any one of their number.[11] How, or whether, this Act worked is not known, but it lapsed in 1510 and was not renewed. The naming of councillors to serve on commissions, a practice which steadily increased as the century advanced, may also have been partly directed at this problem. However in 1542 the onus was shifted by another statute to the justices of assize, and there it remained.[12] From 1543 onward the court of King's Bench also received a transcript of all cases heard before the quarter sessions. It is not apparent that the central court ever acted as a result of receiving such information, but the possibility had a salutary effect.

Justices could be, and occasionally were, removed from the commission for disciplinary reasons. Felony or treason, even if subsequently pardoned, invariably resulted in dismissal. So, too, did serious religious non-conformity. A number of zealous Protestants disappeared from Queen Mary's commissions, although the reason was not openly avowed and they were never indicted for heresy. In Elizabeth's reign, as in her father's, all commissioners were required to take the oath of supremacy, and although in the early part of the reign most conservatives fudged the issue in order to keep their places, no conscientious Catholic could do that after the papal bull *Regnans in excelsis* in 1570. There was, however, a great reluctance to dismiss justices for misconduct, even if they had been fined or imprisoned. John Hawarde reported only seven such cases between June 1596 and November 1607, and Lambarde a little earlier noted it as a remarkable occurrence when a justice was 'put out of the commission of the peace by order in the Star Chamber'.[13] The main reason for this seems to have been sensitivity to the loss of face which such a dismissal involved. A few years later, in 1621 'it was propownded [in the House of Commons] that thowgh it was noe disgrace not to be a justice of the peace, yet to bee excluded is a disgrace'.[14] After all, most of the members were justices themselves and understood such feelings. In the later part of James's reign it was felt as a grievance that the Council had carried out a thorough purge of unworthy or unsatisfactory magistrates, some commissions losing as many as twenty members. By that time clearly the pressure of demand had caused the selection process to become seriously relaxed. There are few signs of such problems in the sixteenth century, but in 1621 a special committee of the Privy Council set out some guidelines which clearly indicated what had happened. No justice was to be too young; none were to be worth less than £20 a year in 'the kinges bookes' (that is, the taxation assessment); no lawyer was to be admitted unless he had been a Reader (at one of the Inns of Court); and no clergyman unless he was a bishop, or 'of most gravyty'.[15]

Part of the problem was that the commissions, and particularly the commission of the peace, had become sounding-boards of local politics. Feuding families strove to increase their own membership, and that of their friends, while diminishing that of their enemies. As it was extremely difficult to get a personal enemy removed, competition concentrated mostly upon filling vacancies which had occurred naturally. However, a secondary and more subtle war was waged over the order in which the commissioners were listed. Each commission expressed perceived precedence, starting with peers and Privy Councillors, and ending with the least 'substantial', who was often the newest recruit. Consequently a telling blow could be struck if the head of your own family could be raised in the order, or that of your opponents lowered. In the 1580s and 1590s some commissions were revised every few months in order to accommodate that sort of pressure. Elizabethan Norfolk provides a number of examples of families locked in such combat. We have already noticed the Gawdys and the Lovells, but a more significant contrast in styles is presented by the long-running conflict between Edward Flowerdew and Sir Arthur Heveningham. Flowerdew was a lawyer of some distinction, who had built up his career partly by diligent and patient service, and partly by hard, if not quite unscrupulous, dealings in land. Heveningham was a courtier who hated lawyers and who had no inclination to patient service. Heveningham was sheriff in 1581–2, and Flowerdew accused him of a variety of misdemeanours in office. His violent response to these charges led to his exclusion from the bench at the end of his shrievalty.[16] He got his own back by counterclaiming gross misrepresentation, and substantiated his case sufficiently to get Flowerdew excluded as well. Both were subsequently reinstated, but Heveningham typically revenged himself by a physical assault of considerable gravity, and disrupted the quarter sessions at which his victim attempted to obtain redress. Sir Arther was eventually brought to book by the court of Star Chamber, and ordered to pay £600 in compensation. He paid some, but Flowerdew's executors were still trying to extract the balance in 1596. Sir William Cecil had identified the problem as early as 1564 when he had written:

> with the increase of number of justices of peace in every shyre . . . the conservation of peace hath decreased and by multitude of an undiscret nombre of men named for justices, mayntenance, bracery ryotts and such like have multiplied.[17]

There were two sides to the success story of the commission of the peace, even while Sir Thomas Smith was writing his encomium, and an additional reason why Privy Councillors should have been called upon to inject an element of discipline and control.

Norfolk was relatively close to the centre of power. More remote counties might have more fundamental problems, even as late as Elizabeth's reign. The quarter sessions in Northumberland were regularly disrupted by the perennial lawlessness which spilled over from the border dales. Until 1536 the commission for county Durham was appointed by the bishop, and thereafter the bishop served *ex officio*. As late as 1600 it was being claimed that the clergy were heavily over-represented, and it was probably the Durham commission which was being aimed at when the Council spoke of barring all clergy other than bishops. The Welsh commissions also had features of their own. They were introduced in the wake of the 1536 Franchises Act, and were much smaller than their English equivalents. By the terms of the original Acts there were supposed to be no more than eight in each county, although the same pressures operated as in England, and by 1581 the average size of a Welsh commission was eighteen.[18] The Welsh gentry were quick to see the advantages of the new provision, but there were some constraints. A property qualification of £20 a year in land had originally been stipulated, but in mid- and north Wales there were far too few who satisfied that requirement, and it was set aside almost immediately. Later in the century George Owen alleged that this concession had lowered the quality of the Welsh commissions to an unacceptable degree, but their performance does not seem to have been any worse than that of many English commissions.[19] A more important constraint in some areas may have been the language. Although the Bible and the Prayer Book were translated into Welsh, the Council made no concessions in its dealings with the Welsh justices, and a competent knowledge of English was essential. All official transactions had to be conducted in that language, including the quarter sessions. Interpreters were available for the benefit of litigants who spoke no tongue but their own, but the magistrates were not expected to need such services. The problem in Wales was not that the justices were corrupt or inadequate, but that they were dealing with a much less tractable community than those of lowland England. At a time when courtiers and their servants could still brawl on the streets of London, it is not surprising that jurors were assaulted in Brecon. Welsh juries were also notoriously unreliable. Not only were they frequently intimidated, but their own tribal loyalties were allowed to take precedence over all other considerations. Even when just sentences were passed, they were extremely difficult to enforce against entrenched local interests. It was alleged that the Welsh countryside swarmed with outlaws, whose actual immunity to punishment mocked their nominal status.[20] The English common law was an alien system in some parts of Wales, and what English observers took for mere lawlessness was sometimes a preference for the traditional ways of securing justice, although too many such excuses should not be made. Nevertheless the introduction of the commission of the peace, for all Bishop Rowland Lee's misgivings, was a step in the right direction. It mobilised the most powerful gentry in support of royal authority, in theory at least, and the more they became used to the idea and its benefits, the more effective it became. By the end of the century many of the Welsh justices had been educated outside Wales, and were more acclimatised to the expectations of a wider society.

The supervision of the commissions of the peace, which in England rested with the justices of assize, in Wales belonged to the courts of Great Session. The judges of Great Session, like those of assize, were supposed to be immune to the pressures and loyalties of local politics, and seem largely to have been so. They made strenuous efforts to prevent the corruption and intimidation of juries, but with only partial success. In some recorded cases jurors were beaten up by disgruntled litigants under their very noses. It was for this reason that their authority was backed up by a special royal council, the Council in the Marches of Wales. To the history and jurisdiction of this council we will be returning in due course, but it functioned, among other things, as a regional Star Chamber. In that capacity it dealt with those whose cavalier attitude towards the normal processes of justice undermined the king's peace. The Council varied in its effectiveness according to the personality of its president, but it also lacked one power which might have made a considerable difference. It could not remove justices from the commission. That could only be done by the Privy Council, which was sometimes influenced by other considerations than the best interests of justice in Wales. The Council of the North exercised similar jurisdiction north of the Trent, with the additional justification of the need to defend an open border. The Herbert Earls of Pembroke were the only peerage family resident in Wales, while the north of England suffered from a surfeit of nobles. Neither situation was particularly conducive to domestic peace.

Lambarde noted over three hundred statutes which the justices of the peace were required to enforce, the great majority of them of Tudor origin, and complained that 'stacks of statutes' were breaking the commissioners' backs. However his own *Ephemeris* does not really support that. Poor Law duties were burdensome, but the great bulk of a JP's time seems to have been spent in the traditional pursuit of order; either conducting 'police' enquiries, or in petty and quarter sessions. Only about a third of Lambarde's statutes are ever referred to in existing records, and many of those very occasionally.[21] Some justices undoubtedly worked hard, and the Privy Council encouraged them to divide their counties into appropriate districts – usually groups of hundreds – for convenience in administration. It was desirable, but not always possible, to have justices resident in every part of a large county for the same reason. Neither in Wales nor in England was the behaviour of JPs entirely satisfactory, but it was an affordable system which worked well enough for most practical purposes. It was not until the reign of Charles I that something like a struggle for the control of the commissions developed. By 1640 the justices seem to have believed that they enjoyed virtual autonomy, and deeply resented any attempt by the Privy Council either to control their activities or curtail their numbers. The Council, in its turn, regarded this attitude with deepening suspicion, and redoubled its efforts to impose its own agenda. The resulting rift was a significant factor in the drift towards civil war.

Notes

1. W. C. Richardson, *The Report of the Royal Commission of 1552* (1974).
2. J. D. Alsop, 'The Revenue Commission of 1552', *Historical Journal*, 22 (1979).
3. P. L. Hughes and J. F. Larkin, *Tudor Royal Proclamations*, vol. I (1964) no. 333.
4. Sir Thomas Smith *De Republica Anglorum*, ed. M. Dewar (1982) p. 104.
5. A. Hassell Smith, *County and Court: Government and Politics in Norfolk, 1558–1603* (Oxford, 1974) p. 189.
6. Ibid., pp. 27–41, 181–200.
7. L. Stone, *The Crisis of the Aristocracy, 1558–1640* (Oxford, 1965) pp. 385–445.
8. Smith, *De Republica Anglorum*, p. 106.
9. J. H. Gleason, *The Justices of the peace in England, 1558–1640* (1969) p. 9.
10. R. H. Tawney and Eileen Power, *Tudor Economic Documents* vol. I (1924) pp. 47–53.
11. Statute 4 Henry VII c. 12; *Statutes of the Realm*, vol. II, pp. 536–8.
12. 33 Henry VIII c. 10.
13. Gleason, *Justices of the peace*, p. 63.
14. Ibid., p. 64.
15. Sir Dudley Digges, 'Report from the Committee for limitation of Justices. . .' Gleason, *Justice of the Peace*, p. 64.
16. Hassell Smith, *County and Court*, pp. 192–8.
17. Ibid., p.78.
18. 27 Henry VIII c. 24; 34 & 35 Henry VIII c. 26. Hugh Thomas, *A History of Wales 1485–1603* (1972) pp. 65–6; G. Dyfnallt Owen, *Elizabethan Wales* (1964) pp. 176–8.
19. George Owen, *Description of Pembrokeshire*, ed. Henry Owen (1892–1906) pp. 401, 544, 584, 691.
20. Owen, *Elizabethan Wales*, pp. 176–9.
21. Gleason, *Justices of the Peace*, pp. 96–116.

5   The Parliament

Like most institutions of medieval government, parliament had come into existence to serve the needs of the king. From time to time he needed to consult all, or almost all, the peers of his kingdom, as distinct from those whom he chose to call to Council. Rather less frequently it was also useful to consult those less exalted men who nevertheless had sufficient collective weight and wealth to make their views relevant to the conduct of policy, the gentry and the burgesses. The commons, as they were collectively called, were particularly important if the king was in need of money. From a representative assembly he could glean a pretty accurate idea of how much, and how willingly, they would pay. Armed with that information, he then had to decide how to frame his demand. By the end of the fourteenth century it was normal to initiate money bills in the Lower House, and essential to obtain the commons' consent to taxation. By then it was recognised that in order to call an assembly a parliament at all, the commons had to be present. They did not meet with the lords spiritual and temporal in the main parliament chamber, but in a place apart, which varied with the convenience of the time. The medieval parliament was also a high court, and when it functioned in that capacity, the Lords acted as judges and the Commons as petitioners. It therefore became customary for aggrieved subjects to submit petitions to the Commons for processing in this judicial fashion. The agreed outcome then became an Act, which was the origin of private legislation. Such an Act only became complete and effective when the king's consent was added, which was normally done at the end of the relevant session, the monarch being an essential and integral part of every parliament. Public matters, such as taxation and amendments to the law, which had originated with the king or his councillors, were similarly cast into Acts, but using a slightly different format.[1] The ability of parliament to legislate was clearly recognised by 1400, but it was perceived as a form of judicial interpretation rather than a unique function. Case law was a familiar concept, and it was as judges rather than as representatives of the community that the Lords and Commons were perceived to be legislators.

The king's control over membership diminished gradually as customary forms became established. Peers were summoned by individual writ, and it was never disputed that the king had the right to withhold a summons, even from an undoubted peer of full age, but if Henry VIII considered the attendance of any particular individual to be undesirable, then his writ would not be withheld, but accompanied by a verbal or written message advising him that he was not expected to respond. The same technique came to be employed with the bishops, whose custom of attendance was equally well-entrenched. Only the mitred abbots offered much in the way of genuine flexibility, because although a small number of major abbots were invariably summoned, there was no defined constituency, or certain criteria of qualification. Membership of the House of Commons moved steadily in the same direction. The election of two knights from each shire became established at a very early date, and the king was only one of a number of competing influences in deciding who those should be. Town representation, however, was at first highly flexible. In the thirteenth century the number of towns represented varied from twenty to about a hundred. Although a few major cities, such as York and London always sent members, there seems to have been little constraint upon the king's freedom to designate parliamentary boroughs on an *ad hoc* basis.[2] By the end of the fourteenth century, however, the balance had shifted and most towns which were enfranchised were represented on a regular footing. In 1510, when the House of Lords numbered about a hundred, there were 74 knights representing 37 counties and 222 burgesses from 110 boroughs, the City of London uniquely having four members. The king no longer sent election writs to boroughs through whim or temporary convenience, but it remained his exclusive right to issue the charters which conferred parliamentary status. All the Tudors did this, Edward VI and Mary being particularly active, and borough representation went up from 251 in 1547 to 370 in 1603.[3] There was only one increase in the county membership, from 74 to 90 as a result of the shiring of Wales. Consequently the balance between knights and burgesses changed quite significantly. Meanwhile the House of Lords had declined in numbers, because the secular peers remained constant at about fifty, and although the number of bishops went up from 21 to 26, the abbots disappeared after 1540, leaving the spiritual peers in a permanent minority.

Whether the peers had declined in authority as well as numbers by the end of the sixteenth century is debatable. In general the Tudor nobility had become more biddable, and Elizabeth neither looked for, nor received, much trouble from the Upper House in parliament. The only occasion on which she had much difficulty getting an important measure through was in 1559 when a number of lay peers joined the surviving Marian bishops to oppose the bill of uniformity.[4] However Henry VIII had never had much trouble getting measures through the Lords either, and the only occasion on which the peers were clearly responsible for rejecting a measure which enjoyed the monarch's support was in Mary's second parliament, in April 1554. That episode was mainly the result of a miscalculation by the Chancellor, Stephen Gardiner, and did not indicate that the queen was seriously at odds with her peers. The relationship between the Lords and the Commons, on the other hand, did change. As early as the middle of the fifteenth century membership of the Lower House was coming to be regarded as a perquisite rather than a burden. Gentlemen wished to serve, and wished their sons to follow them, rather in the same manner as on the commission of the peace. This created an opportunity for patronage which the peers were quick to exploit. Not only could counties be pressured into returning members who were of a particular affinity, but the far more numerous burgess places became desirable commodities. Because the electoral system was in most places weak and vulnerable, towns could be cajoled or forced into surrendering one or both of their nominations. At first this increased the control of the Lords over the Commons, and the obstreperousness of the Lower House in the 1450s largely reflected the strength of the opposition to the Beaufort faction in the House of Lords. However, as the Crown gradually diminished the power of the noble affinities, the parliamentary gentry became more independent. By the reign of Elizabeth most peers still controlled some places, and in the case of major courtiers such as the Earls of Leicester and Essex these might reach double figures. But some sixty or seventy clients in a house of nearly four hundred would not have been decisive, even if they had been controlled by a single patron. As it was, such clientage was a factor to be borne in mind by parliamentary managers, no more. Within a generation of

Elizabeth's death voices would be raised in the House of Commons claiming that their lordships were 'but particular persons', while the Lower House spoke for the whole realm. Moreover the Commons could buy out the peers several times over. No such opinion was expressed in the queen's lifetime, and the Upper House retained its premier status, but clientage was used mainly to orchestrate pressure groups, and the Lords could hardly be said to influence the Commons as a whole.

The growing importance of the Commons is not simply a matter of historical hindsight, in spite of the care which needs to be exercised in assessing it. They did not acquire their own chamber until St Stephens Chapel was given to them in 1547, but it was already recognised that salutary if unwelcome voices were more likely to be raised among the lawyer gentry of the Commons than among the Lords.[5] The Speaker was a royal nominee, and controlled the agenda, but he was also the servant of the House, and could be effectively pressurised by determined lobbies. At the beginning of each session the Speaker petitioned the monarch for freedom of speech, not on behalf of individual members, but on his own behalf, to represent the views of the Commons frankly, without fear of royal displeasure. This was invariably granted, because there was little point in convening a parliament and then suppressing the views which it wished to express. However before the end of Henry VIII's reign the privilege had been extended by custom to individuals, provided that what they said was within the precinct of parliament, and addressed to the issue currently before the House. In petitioning for privilege in 1559, Sir Thomas Gargrave specifically asked 'that they might have liberty and freedom of speech in whatsoever they treated of or had occasion to propound and debate in the House', a request which the queen was 'well contented to grant', provided that they were mindful of their duties.[6] Peter Wentworth's notorious speech of 1576 and his questions of 1587 were not so much demanding an unprecedented freedom of speech as endeavouring to insist that the queen should pay heed to the voices of private members when they attempted to counsel her on affairs of state. This was an opinion for which the House was not yet ready, because it went far beyond an issue of privilege, and impinged directly upon the monarch's prerogative to seek counsel wherever he or she chose.

The second main privilege, which arose directly from the function of parliament, was freedom from arrest on private suits, which normally meant debt. This applied to members of both Houses and their servants, and arose from the principle that the king's business took precedence over all private matters. It was controversial, partly because of the difficulty of defining what constituted a servant, and partly because a creditor frustrated in this way could not return to the charge once the session was over, and therefore probably lost his money.[7] Traditionally such privileges had been enforced by a writ out of Chancery, but in a test case in 1542 the House insisted, with the king's full support, in obtaining the release of one George Ferrers, a burgess of Plymouth, from the custody of the sheriff of London by the authority of the mace alone. Thereafter the House successfully claimed a right of discipline over its members and their servants by the same authority, a fact which probably gave rise to the mistaken view that the House of Commons was itself a court of record. In theory control over attendance was strict. Any member wishing to absent himself during a session had to apply to the Speaker for a licence, and the House was intermittently 'called' to detect unauthorised absenteeism. In practice attendance was patchy, because it was recognised that most members had other business to attend to in the capital, but the possibility of punishment was always there, and in 1589 Elizabeth drew the Speaker's attention to the fact that attendance was unacceptably low.[8] There was even a mass exodus towards the end of Mary's third parliament, which has never been satisfactorily explained. Clashes with the courts were not confined to the arrest of members; attendance might be required as a witness or litigant at a distant assize court. In such a case the only answer was a writ of *supersedeas*, and that the House could not issue for itself. Application had to be made to the Lord Chancellor.

Qualification for membership of the House was a grey area. In 1550 it was ruled by the House that the eldest son of a peer was not a nobleman, and was entitled to sit in the Commons, if so elected. Three years later it was similarly ruled that a priest, 'having voice in the Convocation House', was ineligible for that reason, and could not take his seat.[9] However in both cases the return of royal writs was involved, and the Chancellor must have chosen not to intervene. Sir Thomas Bromley exercised similar discretion in 1581 when a case was appealed to him concerning a burgess indicted of felony. He accepted that the jurisdiction was his, but declined to act without the advice of the House, which thereupon decided that the said burgess should continue to sit unless or until he should be convicted.[10] The queen was less complacent, and in 1586 insisted that Bromley should exercise his jurisdiction over a disputed election, 'a thing in truth impertinent for this House to deal withal, and only belonging to the charge and office of the Lord Chancellor' (D'Ewe's Journal). In the event Bromley again accepted the advice of the Commons, but not without drawing attention to the queen's pleasure. By the end of the century the Lower House had established a committee consisting of all the Privy Councillors in the House, plus a number of others, to examine all returns and adjudicate disputes. In less than another generation the Lord Chancellor's jurisdiction had gone by default.

If qualification was sensitive, then confidentiality was even more so, being, in a sense, the condition of free speech. In 1555 several members who were suspected of concerting tactics outside the House were interrogated and committed to ward, it already being a well-established principle that parliament matters were not to be divulged. In 1589 the Speaker considered it to be necessary to remind members of this, and warned them against table-talk, and the passing of notes to outsiders.[11] For the same reason outsiders who were discovered within the precinct were imprisoned, and might be heavily fined. In 1581 servants were positioned to warn off intruders, and in 1593 one Matthew Jones, who had been discovered on the premises, 'appearing unto the House to be a simple ignorant old man', was pardoned upon his humble submission.[12] In spite of their representative function, access to the mysteries of state set the members of parliament apart from their neighbours.

One characteristic of its composition undoubtedly helped to make the English parliament unusually effective. There was no House of Clergy. In other words the church did not constitute an Estate of the Realm, and in that it was almost unique among the representative institutions of western Europe. The bishops and abbots sat in the House of Lords by virtue of their temporalities, not because of their spiritual status, and the lower clergy were relegated to their provincial convocations, which were never part of the parliament at all, although they met by custom at the same time. It is hard to imagine the legislation which created the English

Reformation receiving the assent of all three Houses if one of them had constituted the Ecclesiastical Estate. A major factor in Henry VIII's success in obtaining recognition for the royal supremacy was that both Houses were predominantly secular, and that the members stood to gain significantly from their cooperation. Nor was there any clash of laws. Although some of the bishops were canon lawyers, the House of Lords was presided over by the chief law officer of the Crown, and the House of Commons was dominated by common lawyers who welcomed such a golden opportunity to cripple a rival system with which they had been in dispute for centuries. If the parliament was distinctive in mingling temporal and spiritual peers, it was also unusual in merging gentry and burgesses. This was facilitated by the fact that the English aristocracy was not a caste. Not only was the son of a peer a commoner, but the son of a gentleman might well be a lawyer, or a merchant. The status of a nobleman was distinct in that he enjoyed the right to be tried by his peers, but he was not exempt from taxation, nor from any of the normal penalties of the law, except that he was not subjected to the indignity of corporal punishment, an immunity which he shared with the gentleman. However sensitive the English aristocracy may have been on the subjects of ancestry and coat armour, they were seldom averse to profitable alliances with plebian but wealthy families. They were also substantial investors in commercial enterprises, and the networks of the court and the City of London were closely interwoven. The House of Commons was not therefore divided into two distinct groups, let alone two antagonistic ones.

The use of statute to resolve Henry VIII's Great Matter, and the extremely delicate issue of the succession, not only transformed the status of such established legal instruments, but also greatly increased the workload of the parliament. Between 1529 and 1559 only eight years did not see a session, and six years contained more than one. This level of activity was not unprecedented; it had been equalled over a longer period between 1370 and 1450, but it was in marked contrast with the immediately preceding period, which had seen only six sessions in thirty years.[13] Moreover the quantity of legislation produced was much higher than in the early fifteenth century, and embraced a wider range of issues. By the end of Henry VIII's reign bills were being introduced on every conceivable subject from treason and the exercise of ecclesiastical jurisdiction to the manufacture of hats and caps or the paving of streets in some particular town. Many of these were officially sponsored, and might be introduced by members of the king's Council in either House, but many more were promoted by the particular interest groups which they affected. Such measures often turned into Acts as much by the indifference of the majority as by the zeal of the promoters, and were sometimes swiftly repealed or amended as soon as their impact had alerted other interested parties. The processing of bills became a highly skilled and expensive professional activity, and one much in demand.[14] The outlines of parliamentary procedure were already well-established before 1485, but as the needs of both private interest groups and the councillors who managed the Crown's business became more precise and complex, so the structures of procedure filled out and developed. It was already normal before the end of the fifteenth century for bills to be read three times in each House, and approved in each, before being sent for the king's approval. However it was quite possible for contentious bills to be read more often, and such measures were not infrequently withdrawn and resubmitted in an amended form. To reduce the need for this, and to facilitate the process of amendment two changes were introduced. During the reign of Henry VIII bills began to be presented on paper instead of parchment, and only engrossed after the second reading. Bill committees, very rare before the sixteenth century, also began to be used with some regularity. Promoters consequently had to be persistent if they did not wish to see their bills stuck or sidetracked, and at each stage fees had to be paid to the relevant clerks.

The rules of debate, which applied equally in both Houses, were already well-established by the end of Edward IV's reign. Speakers must address the chair, and their language must be decorous. In formal sessions, although not in committees, a member might only speak once at each reading of the same bill, and he must desist if required to do so from the chair.[15] In practice debates were not as orderly as these rules might suggest, and discourteous demonstrations of dissent were common, but the kind of violent and disorderly conduct which marred some sessions of the Commons in the early seventeenth century is not known to have occurred. Before the sixteenth century divisions in the formal sense

seem to have been unknown, although differences of opinion must
have been expressed. Some certainly took place during the reign of
Henry VIII, and it may have been then that the rules were devised.
In the Lords every peer's vote was individually recorded, and
proxy votes were allowed. In the Commons decisions were at first
reached by acclamation, but it soon became clear that this
favoured the louder voices rather than the greater number. By
the middle of the century it was normal for the ayes to leave the
chamber, while the noes remained seated. In a small chamber like
St Stephens Chapel this inevitably favoured a negative decision
because the uncommitted would be reluctant to lose their seats. As
the pressure of business grew and the issues became more complex,
the number of committees multiplied. Some of these were standing
committees for a session, like that which coordinated private bills in
order to prevent the Houses discussing a variety of bills on the same
issue. *Ad hoc* committees dealt with matters of privilege or internal
discipline, and sometimes looked at issues raised during debate, to
determine whether legislation was necessary.[16] Apart from specific
bill committees, all these practices seem to have developed during
and after the Reformation Parliament, increasing markedly during
the reign of Elizabeth. All these were single House committees.
Joint committees of the Lords and Commons were usually termed
'conferences', and had existed intermittently since the fourteenth
century. These were usually intended to prevent misunderstanding
or the possibility of conflict, but they offered opportunities for the
better-informed Lords to instruct their colleagues as to the nature
of the king's pleasure and intentions. This was hardly necessary
after 1529, but conferencing grew in frequency until the latter part
of Elizabeth's reign, when an increasingly crowded parliamentary
timetable seems to have squeezed it to the margins. By the 1580s it
was normal for sessions of the Houses to be held in the morning,
with the afternoons devoted to committee work. Such heavy
demands upon their time did not please some members, and
Commons committees became increasingly large to deal with the
growing problem of non-attendance. No Speaker's licence was
needed to skip a committee! By 1600 the Commons also had a
device called the Committee of the Whole House, which any
member was entitled to attend, but over which the Speaker did
not preside. The reason for this development is debatable, but it

was probably intended to facilitate ordinary business, rather than to provide members with an opportunity to criticise the queen behind the Speaker's back.[17]

Parliamentary procedures undoubtedly became more sophisticated, and more strictly enforced, after 1509. But it must also be realised that we know this very largely because the Journals of the House of Lords commence in 1509, and those of the House of Commons in 1547. The first parliamentary diaries partly cover the sessions of 1571 and 1572, but it was not until the very end of the reign that private members began to keep the kind of notes which are so very informative for the Long Parliament. Sir Symonds D'Ewes made a paraphrase of all the journals of both Houses during Elizabeth's reign, but that is mainly valuable for the period 1584–1603, when the original Commons Journal is missing. The parliament rolls of the later Middle Ages offer very full information about the business which was brought before the Houses, but none at all about how they dealt with it, which can be only very patchily reconstructed from circumstantial accounts.

In normal circumstances the monarch attended parliament only at the opening and closing of each session, on the latter occasion granting or withholding assent to the legislation which the session had generated. In November 1554 Philip and Mary took the very unusual step of paying a formal visit in mid-session, in order to assent to a bill restoring the status of Cardinal Pole, so that he could reenter the country while parliament was still sitting. Henry VIII seems to have dropped in from time to time. In March 1531 the Imperial ambassador, Eustace Chapuys, observed casually

> The king had not yet been at the parliament since it recommenced, until late yesterday, when he remained an hour and a half or two hours in the House of Lords, and did not go down to that of the Commons.[18]

In 1532 he is supposed to have been present 'in both Houses to see his supporters win', but the reason, if not the fact, is hypothetical. None of the later Tudors followed their father in this practice, although all received parliamentary delegations from time to time, an experience which the members involved often found distressing. Mary gave such a delegation the rough side of her tongue in November 1553 when they presumed to petition her about her marriage, and groups who waited upon Elizabeth often left with their ears burning. Parliament did, however, provide a very good platform for a monarch who wanted to say something of particular importance. Normally the Lord Chancellor made the closing oration, but his function could be usurped. In December 1545 Henry closed what was effectively his last parliament with a valedictory speech, praising the 'good estate of the Lords and Commons', as well he might considering what they had enabled him to do. In a more defensive mode, Elizabeth did a very similar thing in her 'Golden speech' of December 1601, which was essentially a damage limitation exercise in the grand manner.

The Tudors might harangue their parliaments, but they did not expect to have to manage them themselves. That was a matter for the Council, or, more accurately, for particular councillors. The more important statute became, and the more widely it was used, the more pervasive and complex the problems of management became. Very little is known about how the Council of Henry VII addressed them. Before 1500 there was a general consensus in support of the king, as being the only real guarantor of stability, and after 1500, when his fiscal policies began to attract serious criticism, there was only one parliament to express it. Wolsey was seriously unpopular with both the Lords and the Commons, and on the only occasion when he was forced to face a parliament, his bullying tactics were resented and unproductive. The story of management really begins with the Reformation Parliament, and relates mostly to the House of Commons. The Lords were more closely in touch with the court, and a sizeable proportion of them, both spiritual and temporal, owed their status to the monarch in possession. It was possible, but seldom necessary, to create new peers, or instruct old ones to stay away, in order to create a majority. The closest call was in 1559, before the bench of bishops had been reconstructed, but managing the House of Lords was an aspect of managing the whole noble estate, and best carried out on the basis of personal communication. The Commons, on the other hand, were not biddable in the same way. A few members sat for boroughs of which the king was patron, and they could be nominated if the Council was so inclined, but in principle all counties and boroughs were supposed to enjoy 'free' elections. When Thomas Cromwell was seeking a seat in November 1529, he approached Ralph Sadler, who approached John Gage, who in

turn spoke to the Duke of Norfolk, who controlled several boroughs. When Norfolk had consulted the king, the message came
back 'that his Highness was very well contented ye should be a
burges, so that ye would order yourself in the said room according
to such instructions as the said Duke of Norfolk shall give you from
the king'.[19] He was not the only member to be placed in this way,
but that sort of control only extended to a small minority of places.

Whether Cromwell learned the lesson of this experience we do
not know, but he seems to have been the first royal minister to
attempt the systematic influencing of elections with the intention of
creating a 'government party' in the Lower House. In 1536 he
negotiated with patrons, both noble and non-noble, to secure the
return of selected individuals, and peremptorily ordered the mayor
and burgesses of Canterbury to annul the legitimate election which
they had just conducted and to return two different men in
accordance with the king's instructions. Evidence of such dealing
creates a bad impression in the modern mind, and led to the belief
that Henry VIII 'packed' the House of Commons. Perhaps the
king, or Cromwell, would have liked to control the majority of
returns, but he lacked the capacity to do so. The intention was to
ensure the presence of a team of effective spokesmen, who would
talk down dissent, rather than of a majority which would vote it
down. Closely counted divisions were almost unknown, and it
could in any case be assumed that a large proportion of the
members would accept what was clearly the king's will without
any special effort having to be made to coerce them. Later regimes
were much more tentative than Cromwell. In 1547 the Council was
almost apologetic about asking Sir Thomas Cheney, the Lord
Warden of the Cinque Ports, to secure the return of Sir John Baker
for Kent, and in 1553 confined itself to advising sheriffs generally
that they were expected to ensure that 'men of learning and
wisdom' were elected. Mary's Council, concerned as it was about
gentry dissent, did no more in 1555 than urge the return of men of
'the wise, grave and catholic sort' to a House which would turn out
to be one of the most troublesome of the century.[20] Elizabeth's
Council did the same almost as a matter of routine, but was also
careful to ensure that courtiers and other patrons were, wherever
possible, mobilised in support of official policy. Given the puritan
proclivities of many of them, this was not always easy, and as
divisions became more numerous voting strength began to matter,

but the manipulation of elections was never the most effective way of ensuring the passage of the government's programme. Any thought of organised groups voting to a common pattern or in accordance with instructions should be abandoned in respect of the sixteenth century. Few patrons were interested in more than one issue, and few groupings would hold together over a range of business. Elizabeth's councillors also had the problem of trying to keep their mistress on a steadfast course. The queen was notorious for her procrastinations and inconsistencies, and her parliamentary managers were not above manipulating debates in the House of Commons in order to convince her of the necessity for purposeful action. In this process their own clients and men of business featured prominently.

The most effective management was that which was deployed in the preparation of business before the session began, and in organised presentation. Wolsey was unprepared in 1523, and did not know how to respond when his intentions were challenged. Cromwell was always careful to have a schedule of draft measures, which could be introduced in order of priority, or when an appropriate opportunity presented itself.[21] The first clear evidence of this happening is in 1532, and it was standard practice by 1540. Every parliament thereafter was similarly prepared, often by a special committee of the Council set up for that purpose. The drafting and redrafting of bills also continued during the session, as the councillors responsible for particular measures reacted to criticism, in committee or on the floor of the House. It was essential to have enough well-briefed councillors in each House to handle challenges of this kind before they began to sway opinion too far, and to have a strategy agreed with the Speaker, so that these councillors could deploy their arguments most effectively within the rules of debate. When it appeared likely that the burgesses of King's Lynn and Coventry would talk out the chantries bill in the parliament of 1548, the councillors in the Commons persuaded them to desist by offering exemption clauses for those two towns, which had the desired effect. Another technique was that so energetically deplored by Peter Wentworth in 1576:

> Amongst other, Mr. Speaker, two things do great hurt in this place, of the which I do mean to speak. The one is a rumour that runneth about the House, and this it is 'Take heed what you do;

the Queen's Majesty liketh not such a matter; whoso preferreth it, she will be offended with him': or the contrary, 'Her Majesty liketh of such a matter, whosoever speaketh against it, she will be much offended with him.' The other: sometimes a message is brought into the House, either of commanding or inhibiting, very injurious to the freedom of speech and consultation.[22]

Such rumours and messages were not a new development in Elizabeth's reign, but they were characteristic of her style of management, and Wentworth did not speak for the majority of his colleagues in resenting them. Most members probably welcomed an indication of what was expected of them before making their opinions public. Every public measure was introduced by a councillor, and since the order of speaking in debate was determined entirely by the Speaker, it was not difficult to ensure that all the other councillors present made their contributions. It was also normal for a senior councillor in the Commons to propose a name for the election of the Speaker, a name which was invariably accepted. Modern notions of 'free election' were no more relevant in the House than in the constituencies. When either House was troublesome, it meant that Council management had for some reason broken down. This happened in the Lords in 1554, when the councillors were at odds among themselves, and in the Commons in 1555 when the councillors present lacked the experience, and perhaps the intelligence, to outwit an opposition which included Sir William Cecil. The fact that such cases are notorious also indicates how rare they were. The Tudor Council normally managed its parliamentary business with considerable efficiency.

Opposition to the monarch's wishes over particular issues certainly existed, but not an opposition in the modern sense. Before the reign of Elizabeth grumblings of dissent were almost invariably about money, or property rights. In 1523 it was reported that 'there hath been the greatest and sorest hold in the Lower House for payment of two shillings in the pound that was ever seen, I think, in any parliament'.[23] The first version of the bill of uses was vigorously opposed in 1532, and substantially modified in consequence, whist the notorious rejection of the 'exiles bill' in 1555 was brought about, not by sympathy for the plight of Protestants in Germany, but lest it should create a precedent for the confiscation of real estate without due process of law. Members expressed their unhappiness with Henry's treatment of Catherine, and their unease about Mary's decision to marry Philip, but they did not venture to oppose the royal wishes directly. Even the radical religious policies of Edward VI's Council, which certainly ran counter to the wishes of the majority, were not resolutely opposed in either House. Mary's decision to return first-fruits and tenths to the Church was only passed on a division, but that again was a property issue, and there was no division over the request for papal absolution. After 1558 the position began to change somewhat. The bills for the restoration of the royal supremacy and the protestant settlement were passed only after divisions in the Lords, the latter very narrowly, but thereafter the differences were over strategy and tactics rather than aims. Some members of the House of Commons became deeply dissatisfied with the pace of the queen's programme of religious reform, and kept up a barrage of exhortation and criticism which Elizabeth found profoundly irritating. Her inter-mittent attempts to silence this onslaught were probably mistaken, in that they raised issues of privilege which united the Commons behind a group which was probably never more than a vocal minority. Other matters, such the queen's marriage, the succession, and the fate of Mary Queen of Scots, also drove members of the Lower House to offer Her Majesty a lot of unsolicited and unwelcome advice. Whether this should be classed as opposition is a moot point, because it nearly always took the form of attempts to introduce measures which the queen was constrained to stop, rather than the obstruction of bills which she wished to see passed. What is clear is that by 1601 members of parliament felt perfectly entitled to hold, and promote, their own views about what constituted the good of the commonwealth. The Lords had always believed that – it was a function of their status – but in the Commons it was something new, and the substance behind Wallace Notestein's now discredited thesis about the 'winning of the in-itiative'.[24]

The main purpose of government was to preserve 'the good quiet and prosperous estate' of the commonwealth. In the sixteenth century this was a burden laid chiefly upon the monarch, but parliament was a principal means to that end. Consequently everyone had an interest in its doings, either directly or indirectly. Taxation, for example, had begun as an extraordinary aid granted to the king when he went to war, but by the middle of the Tudor period the parliamentary subsidy was accepted as a proper means of mobilising the private wealth of the country in support of the necessary functions of justice and administration. The former cry that the king 'should live of his own' was no longer heard. Although individuals might seek to evade it, in whole or in part, the payment of taxes was recognised as a normal duty of citizenship, and one of the functions of the king's Council was to ensure that the relevant subsidies were voted, assessed and collected. It raised a storm in 1637 when Chief Justice Finch ruled in Hamden's case that no Act of Parliament could 'bind the king not to command his subjects, their persons and their goods', but a tax duly voted was a binding obligation. The subsidy Acts set out the rates to be paid, stipulated the instalments, and authorised the commissions or other methods to be used for assessment and collection. Elections, as we have seen, provided regular occasions for local politics to interact with those of the court and Council, and the sessions brought men to London who would not otherwise have had occasion to make the journey. The burgesses of Newcastle and Exeter rubbed shoulders with gentlemen from the midlands and the Home Counties. Some members served regularly over long periods and these 'old parliament men' formed business and marriage connections which far transcended their local communities. For a similar reason membership of the House of Commons was often a stepping stone to royal service. Ambitious men, particularly lawyers, used the opportunities of debate to get themselves noticed. Henry VIII certainly paid attention to what was said, and it was alleged that he would 'in the parliament time, in his weighty affairs [ask] if Petite were of his side', referring to John Petite, a London burgess of great experience and integrity.[25] Thomas Cromwell's search for a seat in 1529 was almost certainly part of his campaign to move from the service of the discredited Wolsey to that of the king. As Sir Geoffrey Elton noted 'by the 1530s membership of the House of Commons was something which men with political ambition could and would use as a stepping stone in their careers.'[26] By 1551 about a quarter of the Privy Council had entered royal service by that route.

The omnicompetent nature of statute not only prompted powerful interest groups, like the City of London, to promote legislation, it also attracted large numbers of private individuals hopefully seeking their own interests. The Marquis of Northampton resolved his tangled matrimonial affairs by that means in 1551, and the elder Sir Thomas Wyatt promoted two successful bills in the parliament of 1540. In 1534 Sir Richard Whethill endeavoured to secure a statute confirming a promotion in the Calais garrison, which he had secured in face of the Lord Deputy's determined opposition, but Lord Lisle's parliamentary tactics were superior to his own, and he was defeated. The largest number of bills directly relating to the affairs of private individuals was actually introduced in the reign of Henry VII, but these were mostly restorations in blood arising from the turmoil of the previous twenty years. Henry VIII's parliaments averaged about eight or nine such Acts per session, and those of Elizabeth a little over thirteen. Since the failure rate of such bills was high, these figures must represent a very much larger number of attempts, perhaps as high as forty or fifty per session. Far from being an Olympian institution, parliament was a forum for every kind of daily business from every part of the country, and consequently a major force of unification.

Notes

1. Sir Thomas Smith, *De Republica Anglorum*, ed. M. Dewar (1982) pp. 84–5.
2. G. R. Elton, '"The Body of the Whole Realm": Parliament and Representation in Medieval and Tudor England' in *Studies in Tudor and Stuart Politics and Government*, vol. II (1974) pp. 3–18; M. A. R. Graves, *Early Tudor Parliaments* (1990) p. 5.
3. A. G. R. Smith, *The Emergence of a Nation State, 1529–1660* (1984) p. 387.
4. N. L. Jones, *Faith by Statute* (1982) pp. 129–51.
5. Graves, *Early Tudor Parliaments*, pp. 62–6.
6. Sir Symonds D'Ewes, *The Journals of all the Parliaments during the Reign of Queen Elizabeth* (1682) pp. 16–7.
7. G. R. Elton, *The Tudor Constitution* (1982) pp. 261–2.
8. D'Ewes, *Journals*, p. 453
9. *Commons Journals*, ed. T. Vardon and T. E. May, vol. I, pp. 15, 27 (London, 1852).
10. D'Ewes, *Journals*, p. 283.
11. Ibid., p. 432.
12. Ibid., pp. 511–12.
13. *Handbook of British Chronology* ed. E. B. Friyde, etc. pp. 563–72 (Royal Historical Society, 1986).
14. Graves, *Early Tudor Parliaments*, pp. 47–50.
15. Smith, *De Republica Anglorum*, pp. 82–3.
16. Elton, *The Tudor Constitution*, p. 252.
17. S. Lambert, 'Procedure in the House of Commons during the Early Stuart Period', *English Historical Review*, 95 (1980), pp. 753ff.

18. James Gairdner *et al.* (eds), *Letters and Papers of the Reign of Henry VIII*, (1862–1932), vol. V, no. 120.
19. R. B. Merriman, *The Life and Letters of Thomas Cromwell*, vol. I (1902) pp. 67–8.
20. J. Strype, *Ecclesiastical Memorials* (Oxford, 1820) vol. III, p. 245; J. Loach, *Parliament and the Crown in the Reign of Mary Tudor* (1986) pp. 128–58.
21. Elton, *The Tudor Constitution*, pp. 290–3.
22. D'Ewes, *Journals*, p. 237.
23. H. Ellis (ed.), *Original Letters Illustrative of English History*, 3rd series (1824–46) vol. I, i, pp. 220–1.
24. W. Notestein, 'The winning of the initiative by the House of Commons', *Proceedings of the British Academy*, vol. II (1926) pp. 125–76.
25. J. G. Nichols (ed.) *Narratives of the Days of the Reformation*, 77 (Camden Society, 1859) pp. 25–6.
26. G. R. Elton, 'Points of contact: the Parliament', in *Studies*, vol. III (1983) p. 20.

6   The Royal Court

The court was a magnet which attracted men and women from all over the kingdom. Henry VII did not forget his Welsh roots, and every St David's Day his Welsh servants were given forty shillings to assist with their celebrations.[1] When Henry VIII took his huge following to the Field of Cloth of Gold, every English county was represented among the gentlemen of his train. However, the court did not rely for its impact simply upon its power to attract, it also moved about. This mobility varied greatly from one reign to another. Henry VII had commenced his reign by making a Grand Tour of the realm, going north by way of Lincolnshire to reach York in March 1486, and returning by the western route, going as far south as Bristol. The purpose of this journey was mainly to show himself to his new subjects, and encourage them to make their personal submissions, if they had previously been in the service of Edward or Richard. Henry VIII moved restlessly, but mainly in the south and east of the country. He hardly ever ventured further west than Portsmouth, and only once went north of the Trent, when he visited York in 1541. Edward VI made only one progress during his relatively short reign, and Mary made none at all, although she did travel to Southampton in July 1554 to meet her bridegroom, and to Dover in August 1555 to see him off. Elizabeth made regular and famous progresses, but seldom went far outside the Home Counties. The most notable exceptions were to Kenilworth in 1575 and to Norwich in 1578. Progresses were a matter of policy. They were expensive and sometimes extremely inconvenient, but they stimulated loyalty, and both Henry and Elizabeth loved the demonstrations of enthusiasm and affection which they generated.[2] Regular movement, however, was a matter of necessity. A vast household of some three hundred to four hundred people soon overstretched the primitive waste disposal systems, and the great palaces became foul and unhygienic. Consequently the court moved in a regular but fluctuating orbit around London, utilising some half-dozen large palaces and a number of smaller houses, each of which was kept by a skeleton staff when not in use.

Henry VIII had a prodigious appetite for houses. He inherited nineteen from his father, varying from much-frequented residences such as Richmond and Westminster to hunting-lodges like Ditton and Ewelme, which were seldom if ever visited. Only one of these properties was situated in London itself, and one in Middlesex. Three were in Surrey, four in Oxfordshire, two in each of Kent, Essex and Berkshire, one in Buckinghamshire, one in Northampton, and one far away in Worcester.[3] Many of these Henry VII never saw, and several were leased out, but his son was a conscientious tourist, and visited most of them at one time or another. Henry VIII built five houses from scratch, three of which, Bridewell, St James's and Nonsuch, could be described as palaces. Nonsuch was a remarkable *tour de force* of the early English Renaissance style, and the king was so keen to complete it that he had the builders working all night at one stage. It seems to have been a rather crude imitation of the Château of Chambord, but nothing of it now remains as it was demolished in the late seventeenth century.[4] No fewer than 26 properties were acquired by purchase, exchange or forfeiture, including the palaces of Hampton Court and Whitehall, both from Wolsey. A further twelve were retained after the dissolution of the monasteries. None of these was of major importance as a residence, but they did include the two 'King's Manors', one in York and one in Newcastle-upon-Tyne, later assigned to the use of the Council of the North. The great majority of these premises were kept in regular use, and regularly repaired and maintained by the office of the King's Works, which underwent a major expansion during this period. Tens of thousands of pounds were spent in this way, and on major extensions and improvements. The king did not use even a quarter of these houses on a regular basis. Some he visited only once or twice in nearly forty years; others were assigned to the use of his consorts or his children, but almost all were used, providing household employment and a demand for goods and services in the communities in which they were situated. Henry made a habit of using his own houses when on progress, particularly after he had dissolved the monasteries which had regularly provided hospitality in the early years of his reign.

After 1547 the level of activity and expenditure sharply diminished. Edward VI alienated thirteen of his father's houses, although of those only Hatfield and New Hall were residences of any significance. Five of these subsequently reverted to the Crown. Most of the remaining premises were kept in repair, although only a few of them were used by the king himself. Two, the More and Mortlake, are known to have fallen into ruin, and were not subsequently used. Edward acquired only one house, but that was Somerset House in the Strand, retained after the attainder of the Duke of Somerset in 1551. Mary sold, granted or otherwise disposed of eleven properties, two of which were returned to bishoprics and two, Dartford and Syon, restored to religious use.[5] She did not retain any of the acquisitions resulting from the attainders of the Dudleys and the Greys. Elizabeth resumed Dartford and Syon, but again the story during her long reign was one of disposal and dilapidation. Ampthill was partly demolished in 1567, while Clarendon and Enfield were allowed to fall into decay. Four properties, none of major significance, were alienated, while nothing was either built or purchased, and the houses acquired by the attainders of Norfolk, Northumberland and Essex were not retained. The last Tudor did, however, maintain all the major palaces in good repair, using most of them on a regular basis, and the Works accounts show that money was spent on the maintenance of at least ten of her lesser properties, including the King's Manor at both York and Newcastle. Elizabeth left it to her subjects to build in the grand manner, and such 'prodigy' houses as Holdenby, Theobalds and Hardwick were built largely to attract her attention and presence. She made a regular habit of staying with, or visiting, noblemen and gentlemen in the course of her progresses, and although the honour was extremely expensive to the recipient, there was no shortage of competition.

The royal household was not only a major employer, it was also an important consumer, particularly of foodstuffs. Some three hundred people were entitled to bouge of court at the end of Henry VIII's reign – that is, to be fed at the royal tables – but the actual number provided for daily was much greater. This was partly because of a loosely interpreted duty of hospitality, and partly because of the waste and inefficiency which were inevitable in an institution aiming at magnificence rather than economy. By the 1560s, in spite of Cecil's constant representations, it was common for the meals provided for the public tables in the Queen's Chamber to be sent away almost untouched, while courtiers clamoured and intrigued for 'room service' – the unauthorised provision of meals in their private apartments.[6] The Chamber and kitchen servants connived at this abuse because the surplus food from the Chamber was their perquisite, and if they moved quickly they could sell it in good condition to the licensed victuallers of London and Westminster. It is not therefore surprising that the household consumed several times the quantity of food which should have been required to provide for those entitled. However, this was not an unqualified blessing as far as the suppliers were concerned, because of the system known as purveyancing. Originally an itinerant court had moved from one royal manor to another, consuming the produce as it went. This was followed by a taxation in kind, whereby those household officers whose responsibility it was to take up provisions were entitled to commandeer whatever the king required, and to pay for it what the king might choose. By the fifteenth century these purveyancing rates were always well below the market value, and complaints were numerous and vehement. Moreover, because the court spent most of its time within fifty miles of London, the same counties had to suffer this depredation over and over again. By the early Tudor period two factors modified this oppressive system. In the first place many of the commodities subjected to purveyance, such as grain, beef cattle, butter and cheese, were not particularly perishable and could be brought from a distance. Second, many necessary and perishable foods such as milk, eggs, game birds and salad vegetables, which had to be obtained locally, were not subject to purveyance and had to be bought at the full market rate.

Nevertheless by mid-century the system was in obvious and urgent need of reform. Quite apart from the inequitable nature of purveyancing, the procedures of the Board of Greencloth – the household accounting office – were so ponderous that suppliers had to wait months, and sometimes years, for their money. In 1555 a statute tightened up the administration. All commissions to purveyors were to be limited to six months, and were to specify the county or counties covered. Each commission was also to be restricted to stated provisions and quantities.[7] The suppliers were then given receipts which they had to present to the Board of Greencloth in order to claim payment. No doubt these reforms reduced abuses and exploitation, but it is not clear that they resulted in swifter payment. Nearly twenty years earlier Thomas Cromwell had experimented with county composition agreements, negotiated between the officers of the household and the Justices of the peace. By the terms of such an agreement the county would undertake to supply a given quantity of a specified commodity, or commodities, at the 'king's price'. The county's agents then purchased the produce at the full market price, and sold it to the household at a substantial discount, the balance being made up from a county levy, assessed in the same manner as a subsidy. This method had the great advantage of spreading the financial burden, so that it was not always borne by the same few producers. It also meant that the county was not troubled by purveyors in respect of the commodities compounded for. In spite of their advantages, these contracts were accepted only slowly, probably because of the habitual reluctance to pay any tax, direct or indirect, which was not approved by parliament. By the end of Mary's reign about a dozen agreements were in place, all relating to grain, and Sir William Cecil decided to try and make the system universal.[8] It was slow work. In 1561 a book of composition rates was drawn up, covering a variety of produce, and by the following year a few counties had general composition agreements. By 1590 about twenty counties had composition agreements which were more or less working, and several others had contracts, which they had failed to honour. By the end of the reign general compositions had finally been accepted, and the purveyors were confined to a few fringe operations.[9] This was good for the Exchequer, and must have been good for the counties, but it also meant that areas outside the normal orbit of the court were no longer immediately aware of the contribution which they were making to the sustenance of the queen and her servants.

In the last analysis the court was special because the king was special, no longer an overlord of overlords, but a unique focus of loyalty and patronage. The court was far more than a glorified household; it was the theatre of monarchy, and that was one of the main reasons why Sir Geoffrey Elton found it so hard to define. It attracted, at different levels, scholars, musicians and scientists of international repute; the ambassadors and agents of foreign powers, great and small; the politically ambitious; petitioners and fortune-seekers; quacks and confidence-tricksters; and a veritable army of the vagabond and destitute who strove to survive on its leavings. Elizabeth made it clear that every peer and major gentleman was expected to visit the court from time to time, to pay his respects and register his loyalty. Those who failed to do so, for whatever reason, could expect no favours, and might find themselves under suspicion, especially if they should be in dispute with anyone who did have the ear of powerful courtiers. Refusal to respond to a summons to court was tantamount to treason, as the Earls of Westmorland and Northumberland discovered to their cost in 1569, while unlicensed departure, especially under suspicious circumstances, could be almost as dangerous. The major festivities of the Tudor court were a little like the 'crown wearings' of early medieval kings, occasions to see and be seen. Access to the Privy Chamber was tightly controlled, but these festivities were public events, and even when they were held within the precinct of a major palace, little attempt was made to exclude the uninvited guest. The court was a security nightmare, in spite of the rigid ban on any form of personal violence in the royal presence. Edward VI had £600 stolen from his Privy Purse, and in the dangerous days after 1570 Elizabeth had several narrow escapes from political assassination. The Lord Chamberlain's control was not designed to cover risks of that sort, but to make sure that the monarch was not troubled with unwanted company. Since access was crucial to political success, this was no mere social consideration. Between 1535 and 1540, when Thomas Cromwell was in control, even important councillors like the Duke of Norfolk and Stephen Gardiner found a welcome hard to come by. Elizabeth was less biddable in this respect than her father, and usually made up her own mind whom she wanted to see. This did not include anyone, male or female, who had married without her approval. If that had happened, careful fence-repairing by a third party was called for, as Lord Hunsdon managed to accomplish for his wayward son Robert. However, apart from that, there appear to have been no rules. When the Earl of Essex returned from Ireland without permission, the queen was furious, but when Robert Carey abandoned his post at Berwick, and was warned by every responsible courtier to keep away, he gained access via a minor member of the Privy Chamber, and was welcomed.[10]

Courtiers were actors in the theatre of royalty, not spectators. It was part of their job to help the monarch impress his or her subjects, and dazzle foreign ambassadors. They usually knew too much to be overly impressed themselves. Charles Brandon knew perfectly well that he was a better jouster than the king, but he also knew that he was expected to use his skill to maintain the myth of Henry's invincibility. He did so superbly, and was generously rewarded, not for his indifferent generalship or his non-existent wisdom in council, but for his role as an image-maker and inflater of the royal ego.[11] Both Henry VIII and Mary were keen card-players and gamblers, but whereas Mary nearly always played with her ladies, or councillors if they were available, one of her father's favourite gambling companions was the Sergeant of the Kitchen. Henry was by no means always the fearsome and magnificent person that he liked to be thought. When charged to his face by Sir George Throgmorton with having 'had to do' with both Anne Boleyn's sister and her mother, he could only respond, with obvious embarrassment 'never with the mother'. Elizabeth showed similar clay feet to those who knew her well, both in her uncontrollable fits of bad temper and sexual jealousy, and in the fact that she secretly practised the men's steps of the *coranto* in order to keep fit. Each of the Tudors, with the possible exception of Henry VII, showed a childish streak, both in their choice of amusements and in their lack of emotional self-control, which ill accorded with their dignity and pretensions. Their courtiers and personal servants knew that perfectly well, but there were no *paparazzi* lying in wait in the sixteenth century, and although there was avid speculation about, for instance, the true nature of Elizabeth's relationship with Robert Dudley, it was given nothing substantial to feed upon. The great myths of the Tudor monarchy worked at least as much because people wanted to believe them as because they were assiduously and skilfully promoted.

Both Henry VIII and his great rival, Francis I of France, were an odd mixture of Renaissance prince and knight errant. Both were great admirers of Erasmus, and yet each displayed a bellicosity which he deeply deplored. The humanist scholar Roger Ascham was shortly to denounce Sir Thomas Mallory, the author of the *Morte d'Arthur*, for advocating murder and adultery as aristocratic virtues, but Henry modelled himself on Mallory's heroes, and called himself 'coeur loyale' in the lists. Francis, who attracted the services of no less a renaissance polymath than Leonardo da Vinci, also sought his knighthood at the hands of the Chevalier Bayarde, that flower of medieval courtesy and heroics. Henry VIII's enthusiasm for good Latin, for theology and for cosmography, show him to have had the intellectual interests which earned some, at least, of the plaudits which the Italians bestowed upon him. He founded colleges in both Oxford and Cambridge, and employed the distinguished French hydrographer, Jean Rotz. On the other hand the great showpieces of his court, the masques and the tournaments, belonged entirely to the northern tradition. This was the world of the Holy Grail, of mystic grottos, and of damsels in distress. Each joust was preceded by a pageant entry in which the chief participants appeared in elaborate costumes appropriate to the virtues or vices which they represented, and often riding in elaborately decorated pageant cars. A typical example may be cited from 1512:

> first came in ladies all in white and red silk, set upon coursers trapped in the same suit . . . after whom followed a fountain curiously made of russet satin, with eight gargoyles spouting water, within the fountain sat a knight armed at all points. After this fountain followed a lady all in black silk dropped with fine silver, on a courser trapped with the same. After followed a knight in a horse litter. . .The king was in the fountain and Sir Charles Brandon was in the litter. . .Then suddenly, with a great noise of trumpets entered Sir Thomas Knyvett in a castle of coal black, and over the castle was written The Dolorous Castle, and so he and the Earl of Essex, the Lord Howard and other ran their courses with the king and Sir Charles Brandon, and ever the king broke the most spears.[12]

Henry loved this kind of pageant, which was carefully designed to display both his wealth and his prowess. As a young man he disguised himself in all sorts of ways, particularly for romps like the annual Maying, and Catherine, who was always being 'surprised' by these appearances, played her part with remarkable patience and good humour. It must have required considerable self-control not to recognise the disguised king, when he was a head taller than any other man at court, and generously proportioned, even in his youth.

The later years of his reign, when Henry had retired from the lists and his lightheartedness had departed, saw fewer such events, although they continued to be held on important occasions. Edward VI never reached the age at which a personal appearance in the lists would have been possible. He was taught to run at the ring, and seems to have enjoyed the exercise, but the few tournaments which were staged during his reign do not seem to have aroused his excitement. He preferred watching acrobats. Mary was the only Tudor not to have staged a coronation tournament, and she seems to have remained completely indifferent to Philip's partially successful attempts to use jousting to bridge the gap between his English and Spanish courtiers.[13] He took part himself, being a skilful swordsman, but he lacked both his father-in-law's imposing physique and his talent for self promotion. The English were inclined to laugh at him. The queen, of course, would only have been expected to grace the lists with her presence, but she did not do so, perhaps because she believed herself to be pregnant at the time. It was left to Elizabeth to seize the opportunity which her sister had not recognised. Jousting occupied an important place in the tradition of courtly love, because the knight was always supposed to wear his lady's favour on his helmet, and to lay his trophies at her feet. Catherine of Aragon had always performed this role very gracefully, and by the time she was no longer queen, Henry was no longer jousting. Elizabeth not only loved flattery, she also knew that she had to find some way in which to limit the disadvantages of being a woman and a ruler. Courtly love offered the ideal solution. The queen was perfectly cast as the desired but unattainable mistress, in whose service the knight would risk all and perform wonders. Elizabeth presided at the jousts in the manner of Queen Mab, and her fading physical attractions made no difference to the rules of the game. When, in the late 1570s, Sir Henry Lee decided to link these celebrations with the anniversary of the queen's accession, the Accession Day tilts were born, which became one of the most powerful vehicles of the Gloriana cult.[14]

Court masques, and later performances by professional players, were not public occasions, but tournaments were, especially in Elizabeth's reign when special stands were erected for the spectators, who were charged for admission. Even Henry's great junketing at the Field of Cloth of Gold would have attracted few spectators other than the participants; it was not designed for casual onlookers. State entries, however, like jousts, were spectator occasions. There was always a political message to be delivered. In 1501, when the young Catherine entered London as Prince Arthur's bride, the imagery was complex and sophisticated, replete with images of Anglo-Spanish amity, and designed to prove to the visitors just how advanced the culture of this remote northern island could be.[15] Most of it would have been completely lost upon the citizens of London. When the Emperor Charles V visited his uncle in 1522, the emphasis was again on harmony and partnership. No expense was spared to make this 'summit conference' a success. 'The kinges Palace was so richely adorned of all thinges, that my wit is to dull to describe them, or the riches of the hangyngs, or the sumptuous buyldyng and giltyng of the Chambers', wrote the loyal chronicler Edward Hall,[16] and the enthusiasm of the citizens was stimulated with a generous distribution of free alcohol. Eleven years later not even alcohol could produce a joyous welcome for Anne Boleyn. Her coronation entry was a calculated risk, and in spite of the careful orchestration, it was not the triumphant occasion it was intended to be. Every person of importance who could be coerced or cajoled was there, and making the right noises, but the crowd, so important to the atmosphere of such an occasion, voted with its feet. Not to be beaten, however, within a few days Thomas Cromwell had caused to be published a highly coloured account of the proceedings, designed to persuade anyone who had not actually been present, that the city had gone wild with enthusiasm.[17] There were more ways of capitalising upon a pageant than by attracting actual spectators, and the myth of the king's unfailing popularity had to be preserved. Mary's initial entry in August 1553 was almost the exact opposite: a genuinely joyful occasion which went almost entirely unrecorded. The following year she did better, perhaps because a welcome for Philip could by no means be taken for granted. The Londoners were curious rather than enthusiastic, but the pageantry was well-conceived, and wine flowed from the fountains. An official account was prepared, and issued in several languages, so that all the subjects of the vast Habsburg Empire could understand the triumph which the Prince of Spain had enjoyed in England. In January 1559 Elizabeth adopted a 'belt and braces' technique for her own coronation entry. Like her sister's, it was a happy occasion. Not only was Elizabeth popular, but her unchallenged accession meant freedom from the worrying possibility that either Philip or the Queen of Scotland would put in a counter-claim. The queen did not advertise the fact, but she had quietly mobilised her supporters before Mary's death in case that should happen. However, Elizabeth was not merely celebrating her success; she had a message to convey. Turning her back upon her sister's regime, she intended to pick up the threads which her father and brother had dropped. Each pageant, carefully vetted by the Master of the Revels, each royal gesture and response, was calculated to inform the spectator of the queen's intentions, and to invite his approbation and support. 'Remember good old king Henry VIII', shouted one bystander, who must surely have been a 'plant'. An English bible was presented, which was received with a show of fervent enthusiasm, and a pageant of two contrasting commonwealths symbolised not only hope, but a complete rejection of the immediate past. Unlike her mother's entry 25 years before, this brought out the crowds, and no doubt word of it spread rapidly, but the queen, or more likely Cecil, was taking no chances. Almost immediately there appeared from the press of the royal printer *The Passage of our most dread Sovereign Lady, Queen Elizabeth, through the City of London to Westminster, the day before her coronation*, which missed no promotional opportunity.[18]

Elizabeth's progresses were longer and less intensive exercises of a similar nature, designed for a very much larger and more diffuse audience. Not all the court travelled. The bulk of the service departments would be represented by their head officers, who would take up local labour as needed on a casual basis. The main exceptions to this would have been the kitchen and the stables. Councillors and Chamber servants joined and left the progress in shifts, on a rota basis. The travelling household was counted in scores rather than hundreds, and although the task of moving the queen's furniture and wardrobe from house to house required a formidable number of carts, no English progress ever approached the 20,000 horses which Francis I of France had taken to Bordeaux in 1526. In 1592 Jacob Rathgeb, secretary to the Duke of Wurtemburg, estimated that 300 carts had been required for the progress of that year, and 1,800 horses.[19] In some years the figures may have been higher, but not by very much. Such a large train moved perforce at a sedate pace, some ten or fifteen miles a day, usually with a break of two hours or so in the middle for a meal. This method of progression not only gave the queen maximum exposure to her loyal subjects, it also doubled the number of 'hosting' opportunities, and enabled some of the less affluent gentry to provide limited hospitality without bankrupting themselves. This can be very clearly seen on the East Anglian progress of 1578, for which detailed accounts survive, and was no doubt used on other occasions. The spectators were not just farm workers, drawn from their labours by the passing spectacle. When the queen entered Suffolk, she was greeted by the sheriff, Sir William Spring, accompanied by

> two hundred young gentlemen, clad all in white velvet and three hundred of the graver sort apparelled in black velvet and fair chains . . . with fifteen hundred serving men more on horseback well and bravely mounted . . . which surely was a comely troop, and a noble sight to behold.[20]

This escort, possibly working in shifts, stayed in attendance throughout Elizabeth's journey across the county, which took some three days, and must have involved just about all the able-bodied gentlemen available. It would be no great exaggeration to say that the whole political community of Suffolk had turned out to welcome their sovereign. Norwich, the second city of the kingdom, was the goal and climax of this particular progress, and the queen's reception there was orchestrated by Thomas Churchyard, the master of her own choristers. Whether Churchyard was sent from the court or invited by the city is not entirely clear, but his own statement 'I was the first that was called and came to Norwich about that business' suggests the latter.[21] He arrived in the city about three weeks before the progress, little enough time, as he clearly thought, to lick the provincial performers into shape. He seems to have succeeded remarkably well, but since his own account is the only one that survives, it is hard to be sure. At least no embarrassment was caused, and the queen professed herself delighted. That may have been no more than tact, but as she recalled the experience with pleasure in later years, it was probably genuine. Churchyard operated at two levels. On the one hand he was responsible for the formal pageants, like the greeting at St Stephen's gate, 'most richly and beautifully set forth', where the queen was greeted with songs and with heraldic displays. On the other hand, with his little company of men and boys, he ambushed her as she went about her other engagements, inserting little plays and musical interludes, in a manner which Elizabeth seems to have found delightful, but which did not entirely amuse the dignitaries who were responsible for the itinerary. The most enduring image of Norwich, however, is one for which Churchyard was probably not responsible – that of the master of the grammar school, one Stephen Lambert, delivering a Latin oration. It was, by all accounts, a pompous and pedantic performance of unendurable length, but the queen, who was a connoisseur of latin composition, was gracious in the extreme. 'It is the best that ever I heard', she declared, and gave the orator her hand to kiss.[22] It was a fitting symbol of a highly successful visit, because what really pleased Elizabeth was not the professional quality of the performances, but the evidence of real and enthusiastic loyalty which lay behind them. She had a genuine rapport with her people, which was demonstrated repeatedly in different circumstances, and which could not have been simulated by any amount of courtly artifice.

Norwich remembered 1578 for a long time, and no doubt other favoured places also recalled their visitations with pleasure, but what of the majority of her subjects who never saw the queen in person? What influence, if any, did the court have upon their lives? Ordinary people tended to take their myths uncritically, and received their images of their ruler from crudely illustrated broadsheets and ballads, embellished by the rumours and tales of those who had been there – or at least knew a man who had. Loyalty to the monarch was genuine, even among those who had, or thought they had, good reason to distrust the Crown's immediate agents. The court networks affected the gentry of every shire, but did not extend below that social level. For most people the court was as glittering and remote as a stellar galaxy; something fixed on the distant horizon of their lives, stable and unchanging. To the county elites, however, it was great deal more immediate, and amenable to critical appraisal. Not everyone admired its culture, or wished to seek even the minor promotions which favour might bestow. In the 1530s conservative peers and nobles, even some who had been important courtiers, like Lord Hussey, believed that the king had dishonoured himself and the whole realm by his behaviour. The Pilgrimage of Grace was aimed partly at least to recall Henry to his sense of duty as that was perceived by his critics, and to get rid of the evil councillors (Cranmer and Cromwell) who were rotting the moral fibre of the aristocracy. Towards the end of the century some Puritans felt similarly alienated, although they were usually careful not to criticise the queen herself, remembering that she had brought Israel out of the land of Egypt. Edward Underhill did not feel it necessary to abandon his modest career at the court of Edward VI when he fell under the influence of the preachers, but he did become very self-righteous about the sin of gambling, which must have made him uneasy company.[23] Courts had always been a favourite target for the moralists, and the fact that Antonio Guevara's *Menosprecio de corte* and Lorenzo Ducci's *Arte Aulica* were translated into English was of no particular significance. There was always a taste of sour grapes about such polemic, as there was in Sir Walter Raleigh's famous comment that the court of Elizabeth glowed 'like rotten wood'. Rejection was the exception rather than the rule. For the most part the aristocracy sought to ape the moods and fashions of the court, while minor gentry and burgesses imitated their social superiors whenever they got the chance.

Clothes and manners were probably the first things which visitors to the court noticed, and the first fashions which they emulated on their return home. However, under Elizabeth the Chapel Royal was more important, which explains the agitation of the puritanically inclined at the reappearance of the cross and candlesticks upon the altar at St James's in 1560. The queen's chapel was a means by which she could send out coded messages about her preferred religious practices. Church music might well have disappeared if it had not been for Elizabeth's patronage, and the protection which she was prepared to extend to Catholic musicians such as Byrd and Tallis. The master of her choristers travelled the country seeking for new talent, and many families in cathedral cities far from the capital had their first contact with the court when their sons were whisked away to be trained and educated at the queen's expense. However, the greatest social revolution after the dissolution of the monasteries was the transformation in aristocratic education, and that was brought about almost entirely through the influence of the court. Edward IV's *Liber Niger* exemplifies the traditional culture. The Master of the Henchmen was instructed to ensure that his charges were shown

the schools of urbanity and nurture of England, to learn them to ride clenely and surely, to draw them also to jousts, to learn them to wear their harness; to have all courtesy in words, deeds and degrees.[24]

They would have been taught to read and write in the vernacular, and to understand the Latin of the Church, but apart from that book-learning was for clerks, and unworthy of the attention of a gentleman. A generation later the humanist court poet John Skelton could mock such a regiment for the king's amusement:

> Noble men born
> to learn they have scorn,
> but hunt and blow an horn,
> leap over lakes and dykes,
> set nothing by politics.[25]

Henry VIII had already made it clear that although he might sometimes enjoy the company of such old-fashioned aristocrats, and appreciated their services upon the field of battle, when it came to Council and to affairs of state, something altogether different was required. Sophisticated Italians and subtle Frenchmen needed to be met on their own ground, by intellects equally sharp and prepared. The king had received a humanist education himself, and quickly became bored by minds which lacked either content or training to keep up with him. Richard Pace in the 1520s and Sir Thomas Elyot in the 1530s both warned that if noblemen did not give their sons the kind of education which fitted them for this new concept of service, then the sons of commoners would be preferred before them.

The nobility got the message. Before the end of Henry VIII's reign even the most conservative families were hiring tutors of the new learning, and by Elizabeth's reign the connection between learning and preferment was a commonplace:

> you will be but ungentle gentlemen if you be no scholars; you will do your prince but simple service, you will stand your country in but slender stead, and you will bring yourselves but to small preferment, if you be no scholars.[26]

In this, as in other fashions, the gentlemen followed the noblemen, and court gentlemen were sometimes the pioneers, having more to gain. Sir Henry Wyatt set an early trend which many were later to follow when he sent his son Thomas to the newly founded St John's College in Cambridge, soon after the turn of the century. Although the nobility tended to stick with private tutors, the gentry increasingly turned to grammar schools and to the colleges of Oxford and Cambridge universities to provide the necessary education for their sons. These gentlemen students did not always, or even usually, take degrees. They resided for a year or two, acquired a basic knowledge of classical literature and history and a grounding in Protestant theology, and then proceeded to the Inns of Court where they acquired that knowledge of the law which would be really useful to them as justices and as royal servants in their respective communities. By the 1580s the universities were dominated by such men, and increasingly geared to their requirements, a tendency which only the earnest desire for an educated and preaching clergy held in check. The proportion of graduate clergy steadily rose as the century advanced, but the most significant development was that by 1600 the possession of a university degree entitled the holder to be styled 'gentleman'. The losers by this process were the women of the gentry class, who had commonly shared the intellectual part of their brothers' education. Grammar schools and universities were closed to them, and the advances in female education which the humanists had made in the early sixteenth century were not followed up.

Nevertheless by 1600 the whole aristocratic culture had been changed. Hunting still survived, but the martial arts were now mainly for those who intended to devote their careers to such matters. The chivalric romances of an earlier generation had given way to Tacitus and Thucydides. Every gentleman was expected to have a library, which would contain not only an English bible and a selection of history and theology, but a globe and works of cosmography, both general and particular. A portrait of the queen hung in his gallery, and his ancestors, often in fanciful costumes, adorned the walls. Only in one way did the court undermine what was in other respects a notable achievement of civilisation. In 1577 the first school of fencing opened in London, and within a generation the instinctive violence of the aristocracy had obtained a new lease of life. The cult of the duel never reached in England the epic proportions which it attained in France, but it was dangerous and insidious, and bred in the overheated atmosphere of the court. Elizabeth never acted resolutely against it, and by her death a new generation of young bravos had appeared. Fortunately the new civilian culture proved tough enough, backed by Puritan ethical principles, to make sure that this plague was kept under control, and James I eventually reduced it to an unlawful fringe. At the same time the educational revolution produced a new type of class division. In 1500 the Christmas amusements at Richmond or Thornbury were as boisterous and mindless as those being enjoyed in inn-yards and farmsteads up and down the country. By 1600 the sophisticated entertainments which appealed to educated courtiers and gentlemen were completely lost on their humbler neighbours. The educated and uneducated were beginning to speak different languages, and this was not simply a function of wealth, because there had always been rich and poor. The days were coming when the parson and the squire would be natural allies, because they were the only men in the village who spoke the language of school and university. There was a price to pay for the educational revolution. Nevertheless it was a remarkable, if unplanned, achievement, and one in which the leadership of the monarchy through the court is very clearly established.

Notes

1. BL Additional MS 7099 (Craven Ord Transcripts, 1829).
2. Ian Dunlop, *Palaces and Progresses of Elizabeth I* (1962) p. 132 ff.
3. H. M. Colvin, *The History of the King's Works, IV, 1485–1660* (1982) pp. 1–367. In London, Baynard's Castle; in Middlesex, Westminster; in Surrey, Richmond, Woking and Bagshot; in Oxfordshire, Ewelme, Langley, Minster Lovell and Woodstock; in Kent, Eltham and Greenwich; in Essex, Havering and Wanstead; in Berkshire, Easthampstead and Windsor; in Buckinghamshire, Ditton; in Northamptonshire, Collyweston; and in Worcestershire, Tickenhill.
4. John Dent, *The Quest for Nonsuch* (1962).
5. Colvin, *History of the King's Works*; D. Loades, *The Reign of Queen Mary* (1991) pp. 300–1.
6. *Household Ordinances* (1790) p. 153. D. Loades, *The Tudor Court* (1992) p. 63.
7. Statutes 2 & 3 Philip and Mary, c. 6.
8. Loades, *Tudor Court*, p. 72.
9. A. Woodworth, *Purveyance for the Royal Household in the Reign of Elizabeth* (Philadelphia, 1945).
10. G. R. Elton, 'Points of contact: the Court', *Studies in Tudor and Stuart Politics and Government*, vol. III, p. 47.
11. S. J. Gunn, *Charles Brandon: Duke of Suffolk, 1484–1545* (Oxford, 1988).
12. Edward Hall, *The Unione of the two Noble and Illustre Famelies of Lancastre and Yorke (Chronicle)* (1809) pp. 533–4.

13. R. C. McCoy, 'From the Tower to the Tiltyard: Robert Dudley's return to glory', *Historical Journal*, 27 (1984).

14. R. Strong, *The Cult of Elizabeth* (1977) pp. 129–63.

15. S. Anglo, *Spectacle, Pageantry and Early Tudor Policy* (1965) pp. 56–97.

16. Hall, *Chronicle*, p. 635.

17. *The Noble Triumphant Coronation of Queen Anne, Wife to the most noble King Henry VIIIth* (1533), reprinted in A. F. Pollard, *Tudor Tracts* (1903) pp. 9–35.

18. (1559) reprinted in Pollard *Tudor Tracts*, pp. 356–95.

19. Dunlop, *Palaces and Progresses*, pp. 116–17.

20. Ibid., p. 128.

21. J. Nichols, *Progresses and Public Processions of Elizabeth* (1823) vol. II, p. 56.

22. Ibid., p. 26.

23. 'The Narrative of Edward Underhill', in *An English Garner*, ed. E. Arber (1879–82) vol. IV, p. 87

24. A. R. Myers, *The Household of Edward IV* (1959) pp. 126–7.

25. BL Harleian MS 2252, f. 147; John Shelton 'Colin Clout' (c. 1520) lines 621–5.

26. G. Pettie, *The Civile Conversation of S. Guazzo* (1586) sig. A v.

7 The Special Jurisdictions

The government of Wales underwent more extensive change during the sixteenth century than did that of any other part of the Tudor state. In spite of the turbulent and temporarily successful career of Owain Glyndwr in the early fifteenth century, the political map of Wales in 1485 was very much as it had been in 1300. The present county of Gwynedd and part of Clwyd formed the northern principality, divided into the pseudo-shires of Anglesey, Caernarfon, Merionydd and Flint. About half the present Dyfed formed the southern principality, divided into Cardigan and Carmarthen. The remainder was divided into some two dozen private lordships – the so-called marcher lordships, some of which spilled over into England. The principality had neither commissions of the peace nor parliamentary representation, but was in other respects run on the English model, and its courts used mainly English law. The marcher lordships were autonomous. The king's writ did not run. Their customary courts were held in the name of the lord, and used a mixture of English and Welsh law, which varied with the location and the nature of the community. In spite of the fact that a large proportion of these lordships had fallen to the Crown by 1485, their lawlessness was notorious. There were a number of reasons for this. In the first place there was endemic hostility between the rural population, which was purely Welsh, and the urban population, much of which was of English origin because many of the towns had been planted as English colonies. Second, Welsh law had always shown a relaxed attitude to physical violence, and even homicide. Financial penalties and compensation were normal, similar to the 'wergild' of the old Saxon laws, and English officials believed, probably rightly, that this encouraged blood feuds which had little incentive to stop short of murder.[1] Third, the Welsh law of inheritance did not distinguish between legitimate and illegitimate offspring. This caused deep offence to those imbued with English notions of the sanctity of primogeniture, and led to the false perception that the Welsh did not take marriage seriously. Since the fourteenth century the Welsh gentry had been increasingly inclined to use English land law whenever possible, in order to hold their estates together, and this led to severe tensions within the gentry class, which were also conducive to violent outbursts.

Henry VII tinkered with these problems, perhaps inhibited by the contrary expectations which were entertained by the English and Welsh communities, and almost certainly because he had far more pressing concerns elsewhere. Within the principality he gave equality of status to the native Welsh, which was appreciated as a gesture, but made little practical difference. The remaining autonomous marcher lords were placed under heavy bonds for the effective discharge of their disciplinary functions, but their jurisdiction was not diminished. The example here was set by the king's uncle, Jasper Tudor, Duke of Bedford, who was the most powerful of the lords down to his death in 1495. Henry's other main tactic was to place heavy reliance upon his loyal ally Rhys ap Thomas. Rhys became Chamberlain of both Cardigan and Carmarthen, and Constable of the Crown lordship of Brecknock. These offices, together with a host of lesser ones, gave him magnate status in South Wales, although he was never raised to the peerage.[2] It was perhaps because of Rhys's reliability and enormous influence that Henry never felt it necessary to develop the council which Edward IV had established to run the lordships of his Mortimer inheritance. Sir Rhys ap Thomas died in 1525 at the ripe old age of 76, but even before then Wolsey was casting a critical eye over the state of the marches. It had been his power in south-east Wales, and his lack of discretion about displaying it which had brought the Duke of Buckingham to the block in 1521. Henry VIII had no intention of allowing Rhys's family position to become entrenched, and after his death his offices were bestowed elsewhere, to the deep chagrin of his grandson and heir, Rhys ap Gruffydd.

At the same time, Edward's council, which had been converted into a princely council when Arthur was created Prince of Wales in 1489, but had never developed an effective governmental role, was revitalised. The king's only legitimate child, the nine-year-old Princess Mary, although not given the title of Wales, was sent to Ludlow as its nominal head, while the presidency was given to Bishop Voysey of Exeter.[3] The fact that this happened in the year of Rhys's death was probably coincidence, but it was not chance that bestowed the important Chamberlainship of Cardigan/Carmarthen upon Lord Ferrers, the steward of Mary's household, rather than upon Rhys ap Gruffydd. Wolsey's intention was clearly to strengthen the administration of justice in the marches, and to make the marcher lords answerable to a royal authority closer at hand than London. Mary returned to London in 1529, but the council continued to function in her name. By 1534 a continued lack of success, perhaps attributable to Voysey's weak leadership, had again brought the marches to a high place on the political agenda. Rowland Lee, the Bishop of Coventry, replaced Voysey as President, and at the same time all pleas of the Crown from the marcher lordships were removed into the jurisdiction of the nearest English shire.[4] The Council in the Marches was given a general supervisory role over the investigation and punishment of felony, and armed with this new authority Bishop Lee descended upon the lordships like an avenging angel. According to Ellis Gruffydd over 5,000 offenders were hanged, and although this was almost certainly an exaggeration, his visitation was not soon forgotten. Lee had no opinion of the Welsh, believing them to be incapable of self-discipline and in need of a heavy English hand to maintain even a semblance of order.

For this reason he was strongly opposed to Cromwell's statute of 1536, which finally laid the marcher lordships to rest. The price of dismantling this archaic and inefficient structure was to create in Wales and the marches thirteen full shires on the English model, with commissions of the peace and parliamentary representation. Lee had no objection to the latter, but he could not accept that the Welsh gentry were capable of the same degree of self-government as their English counterparts. In the short term he may have been right, because the problem was not solved, but in the longer term Cromwell's more far-sighted statesmanship was generously rewarded. Elizabethan Wales was not noticeably more lawless than neighbouring parts of England, and the Welsh gentry were fully integrated into the political nation.[5] Far from being brought to an end by this reorganisation, however, the role of the Council in the Marches was actually increased, which indicates that Cromwell's action was not based entirely upon confidence in the Welsh gentry. Armed with standing commissions of the peace and of oyer and terminer, it exercised both common law and equity jurisdiction over the whole of Wales, and the English counties of Cheshire, Shropshire, Hereford, Worcester and Gloucester. A second statute of 1543 specifically confirmed both the nature and the limits of the

Council's jurisdiction, which thus came to rest upon parliamentary authority as well as upon royal commission.[6] Principally it was a regional Star Chamber and Chancery, responsible in general to the Privy Council, but not a branch of it. Cases were referred backwards and forwards between the Privy Council and the Council in the Marches, as circumstances and the personalities involved seemed to indicate. Its common law jurisdiction, however, was much less straightforward, and raises questions about the strategy which the English government was pursuing. The Act of 1543 reorganised the courts of Great Session, which now performed for the counties of Wales the same function as was performed for the English shires by the assizes. The Council did not exercise appellate jurisdiction in respect of either of these systems, and the nature of the relationship was undefined. This meant that the Council could pick up cases which were particularly difficult, or susceptible to local pressures, but it also meant numerous and increasingly frustrating clashes. By the end of the century the common law jurisdiction of the Council on both sides of the border was virtually stalled by the opposition of the circuit courts. The Council also supervised the administrative functions of the justices of the peace, a role originally made necessary by the inexperience of the Welsh justices, and continued because it was often more convenient to get guidance from Ludlow than from London. Uniquely among the institutions of the Tudor state, the Council in the Marches was empowered to use torture in the examination of suspects, a practice otherwise confined to the Privy Council itself. This power seems to have been used very seldom, if at all, and the reason for its existence is not clear. In spite of its problems the Council was seen as the most successful regional agency, and even survived the Civil War and interregnum, being finally abolished in 1689.

Two other regional councils were also created, both entirely within England. About the Council in the West there is little to be said in a survey of this kind. It was set up in 1539 because the destruction of the Courtenays needed to be justified on the grounds that they had created a power base in the south-west which was in danger of escaping from royal control. It was intended to cover the four shires of Cornwall, Devon, Somerset and Dorset, in the same way that the Council in the Marches covered the five English border shires. However, since the reason for its establishment was fictitious, it is not surprising that it was soon discovered to be redundant.[7] After Cromwell's fall in 1540 it was discontinued, and its brief existence really tells us more about Cromwell's campaign against the Courtenays than it does about the state of the south-west. The remaining council, however, was a much more substantial and durable affair. The Council of the North originated in the private council of Richard, Duke of Gloucester, who held vice-regal powers in the north on behalf of his brother, Edward IV. When Richard became king he continued this council under the presidency of the Earl of Lincoln. According to the instructions which were issued in 1484, it was to have

> authority and power to order and direct all riots, forcible entries, distress takings, variances, debates and other misbehaviours against our laws and peace committed and done in the said parts.[8]

But this seems to have meant prerogative rather than common law jurisdiction, and there is no indication that it was intended to supersede the existing courts. Richard's council lapsed with his death, and Henry VII appears to have used no exceptional jurisdiction in the north, apart from the long-established march wardenries. The creation of a group of Fee'd Men in each shire reinforced the direct royal presence in the north, but gave it no sort of institutional shape. It was not until 1522 that Wolsey began to direct his attention to the north. Perhaps a renewed threat from Scotland was the trigger, or perhaps the activities of the Duke of Buckingham had alerted him to the dangers of magnate power in remote parts of the realm. For whatever reason the merits of the Yorkist system appealed to him, and in 1525 a new Council of the North was created.

This was attached to the household of the new Lieutenant, the king's illegitimate six-year-old son, the Duke of Richmond, in the same way as the Council in the Marches was attached to that of the Princess Mary. This council was directly responsible for administering the Duke of Richmond's own lands, and all other Crown lands in the counties of Yorkshire, Cumberland, Westmorland and Northumberland. It also had a general overview of the administration of justice in those counties, in the same manner as the Earl of Lincoln's council had done. However the north was unlike Wales in two important respects. In the first place, behind it lay an open

border with a foreign power, the kingdom of Scotland, and in the
second place it had a powerful indigenous nobility. The existence of
the border created an area of lawlessness, where it was often hard to
tell whether the culprits were English free-booters or Scots mar-
auders, and where English outlaws could often find refuge a few
miles away in the next valley. This problem was addressed by the
so-called 'days of truce', when English and Scottish commissioners
would meet together at a border venue to adjudicate claim and
counter-claim. These commissioners were representatives of the
march wardens on either side, and neither the normal civilian
administration nor the Council of the North had any role in the
proceedings, but both were affected if the arbitration failed, and
violence spilled out of the marches into the lowlands. The northern
magnates – the Percies, the Nevilles, the Cliffords and the Dacres –
were a more serious problem, in that they actively resented the
intrusion of the council as an infringement of their traditional role.
It would probably be fair to say that they sabotaged Wolsey's
council. By 1530 the three march wardenries, which had been
attached to Richmond's lieutenantship, had reverted to local
control. Richmond was withdrawn and his function discontinued.
In that year, when Bishop Tunstall of Durham was appointed
President, the council's jurisdiction was confined to Yorkshire, and
restricted to equity matters. When the lieutenancy was revived in
1533, it was for the benefit of the 6th Earl of Northumberland, and
it appeared that the experiment in direct royal control had failed.

However, it soon became clear that Cromwell was approaching
Wolsey's target by a different route. By 1537, when the Earl of
Northumberland died, he had been pressured into making the
Crown his heir, and the whole Percy interest was temporarily
destroyed. This greatly extended the royal lands in the north,
and other acquisitions were deliberately made for the same purpose. How long it might have taken to establish control by this
method in normal circumstances is difficult to say. In the event the
whole process was accelerated, and the council resurrected in a
much more effective form, as a result of the great northern rebellion
of 1536/7, known as the Pilgrimage of Grace. The Pilgrimage was
the most powerful regional demonstration to be made against any
Tudor government. It was caused by a combination of factors –
resentment against the disinheritance of the Percies, against the
dissolution of the lesser monasteries, against the Statute of Uses,

and against many aspects of Henry's religious and political programme. It embraced court allies of the Princess Mary, like Lord
Darcy and Lord Hussey, powerful regional gentry, clergy and
commons.[9] The Pilgrimage failed for a number of reasons. Its
leaders did not see themselves as rebels, but as good subjects trying
to point out to the king the error of his ways; when he refused to be
persuaded, and they were faced with a choice between fighting and
accepting his limited assurances, they chose the latter. Moreover no
lord of major importance joined them. Had the Earl of Derby or
the Earl of Shrewsbury thrown in his lot with the Pilgrims, the
outcome might have been different, but they all supported the king.
At first it did not appear that the tame conclusion to the demonstration, which at its greatest had mustered 30,000 men, would
produce any significant results at all, but a minor insurrection early
in 1537 gave the king the pretext which he needed to embark upon
a fierce policy of repression. Many of the leaders of the Pilgrimage
were arrested, tried and executed, and the Council of the North
was recreated.

In its new form the council was responsible for the whole of
England north of the Humber, with the exception of Lancashire,
and finally abandoned its household origins. The Crown lands were
no longer managed by its agents, and the office of Lieutenant was
discontinued after the Duke of Norfolk had carried out his punitive
campaign in 1537. Like the Council in the Marches, it was headed
by a President, who was a salaried royal official, first Bishop
Tunstall of Durham, and after 1544 Archbishop Holgate of York.
It consisted of some 16–18 councillors, who were a shrewd blend of
noblemen, gentlemen and lawyers, most of them with northern
interests. It therefore did on a large scale what the commission of
the peace did for a county, that is, commit important local men to
the upholding of the royal authority.[10] The council was armed with
standing commissions of oyer and terminer and of the peace, but
there does not seem to have been the same degree of conflict with
quarter sessions and assizes as occurred in the Welsh marches,
perhaps because there were better communications with the justices
of the northern circuit. Its main function, however, was to act as a
regional Star Chamber, imposing immediate penalties on those
who were in a position to evade or delay the normal processes of
justice. Both Star Chamber itself and Chancery referred northern
cases to its jurisdiction, and it carried out general administrative

supervision of the commissions of the peace. General sessions of the Council were held four times a year at York, but other sessions could be held as needed at the discretion of the President, and might be held at Newcastle, or elsewhere according to the nature of the business to be discussed. Four councillors were to remain continually attendant upon the President, who had full executive power to direct the council's activities. Although its jurisdiction covered the northern marches, the council was very careful not to tangle with the military administration of the wardens, or the captains of Berwick and Carlisle, which were the chief garrisons after the conclusion of the last Scottish war in 1550. The Council of the North was briefly wrong-footed by the rebellion of the northern earls in 1569, and the President of the time, the Earl of Sussex, preferred not to grasp that particular nettle. However, 1569 was hardly even a pale reflection of 1536, and never placed Elizabeth in any serious danger. The council once again benefited from the collapse of active opposition to the Crown. With the Percies broken again,[11] and the Nevilles this time joining them in disgrace, while the Clifford Earl of Cumberland was an unpopular absentee, the northern nobility ceased to be a major factor, either for good or ill. In 1572 the Earl of Huntingdon, a man with no personal interests in the north, and a strong puritan into the bargain, began a 23-year stint as President of the Council, and during that time the north lost most of its intractable and ungovernable characteristics. By 1603, when the border ceased to be a potential problem, Northumberland, Cumberland and Westmorland were well on their way to becoming the Middle Shires.

The remaining special jurisdictions within England were, comparatively speaking, of minor significance. The palatine bishopric of Durham had never presented the kind of problems which we have seen in the marcher lordships of Wales. Although it had been created as a buffer against the Scots, by the sixteenth century it was almost out of reach of the lawless border. Moreover as an ecclesiastical franchise, it was always in the hands of loyal servants of the Crown. All writs ran in the name of the bishop, without reference to Westminster, and he held the pleas of the Crown, but by the Tudor period the bishops were invariably outsiders whose justice was unlikely to be swayed by local loyalties or obligations. The risk at the end of the fifteenth century had rather been that the king was too far away to provide adequate support to his man on the spot, and that the royalist gentry who supported the bishop would be unable to make headway against those whose primary allegiance was to Percy, or Neville, or Lumley. It was probably for that reason, rather than from administrative tidiness, that Durham was included in the Franchise Act of 1536. Tunstall was no doubt greatly relieved not to have the responsibility for appointing justices. He still headed the commission *ex officio* and the direct intrusion of the royal authority strengthened his hand. As a recent historian of the bishopric has put it:

After 1536 Tunstall, now installed as President of the Council in the North and Lord Lieutenant of Durham, together with the loyalist Eure, Bowes and their kind, ruled without challenge.[12]

The palatinate Chancery court, and other courts, survived, some down to the present century, but they no longer signified any degree of jurisdictional autonomy. Only in one important respect did County Durham remain distinctive. It sent no representatives to the House of Commons until the late seventeenth century. Having been brought within the jurisdiction of the Council in the North, in every other respect it was a normal county, but its major role in the events of 1569 must have warned Elizabeth's Privy Council of the dangers of complacency. Chester, as we have already seen, had been in the hands of the Crown for generations, and the Act of 1536 changed little except nomenclature. As in Durham, many of the old forms continued, but more to reflect local conservatism than to express any substance. Cheshire and its boroughs were enfranchised at the same time as the Welsh counties, adding over thirty members to the House of Commons. Until 1569 the county remained under the jurisdiction of the Council in the Marches, but that additional complication was then removed in response to its own petition.

The Duchy of Lancaster was similarly a franchise in name only with one important proviso. The palatinate of Lancaster covered only the county, in the same manner as Chester, but the Duchy held land all over England. After 1399 the Duke's council retained an administrative oversight of these lands, and received petitions from Duchy tenants. By the early sixteenth century the principal function of this council had become that of an equity court, and it became known as the court of Duchy Chamber, discharging similar functions to those of Chancery for its more limited clientele.[13] The Duchy Chamber also handled the revenues from the lands under its control, and pioneered the accounting methods later adopted by the court of Augmentations. It survived all the financial reorganisations of the reigns of Edward VI and Mary, and retained its independence into the following century. Several other jurisdictional anomalies also survived, presumably because the vested interests which protected them were somewhat stronger than the council's desire for uniformity. None of them could be judged to have political significance by the Tudor period. One of these was the Stannaries, the court of the Cornish tin miners. The tin miners were a privileged commercial company who had been granted exclusive rights to extract and refine the ore, which had once been one of England's most valuable exports, and was still an important commodity in the sixteenth century. Both the processing and the marketing of tin were subject to strict controls, and the tinners were answerable only in their own courts. The Stannary Court thus handled pleas of the Crown as well as party issues, but by the sixteenth century the Warden in whose name the court was held had become a Crown appointment, so again the franchise was more a matter of form than substance. In the 1590s the position was held by Sir Walter Raleigh.[14] A somewhat similar fate had befallen the much larger franchise of the Cinque Ports. This federation, originally comprising the five towns of Hastings, Dover, Hythe, Romney and Sandwich, had expanded by its heyday in the late thirteenth century to embrace nearly forty towns and villages along the southeast coast, from Seaford in Sussex to Brightlingsea in Essex. It had been created to provide ship service for the Crown, along the same lines as military tenure, and in return the Crown granted the towns extensive commercial privileges and virtual jurisdictional autonomy.[15] The situation was complex, because each town had its own charter in addition to the collective grants of 1204, 1252 and 1260. However, the important privilege from the point of view of this survey was that the free citizens of the Cinque Ports could only plead and be impleaded at the franchise court of Shepway. This had begun as something analogous to a county court, but by the late thirteenth century had also taken over the functions of the General Eyre. By the sixteenth century the prosperity of the towns was long past its peak, and their contribution to ship service was negligible, but the Shepway court still held pleas of the Crown, and no citizen could be impleaded elsewhere. This was a jealously guarded privilege, and was no doubt both practical and useful to those who enjoyed it, but it did not amount to freedom from royal control. Already by the fourteenth century the Shepway court was convened by the Lord Warden, and functioned in his name. Like the Warden of the Stannaries, the Lord Warden of the Cinque Ports was a Crown appointment, which was linked to the constableship of Dover Castle. However independently they may have acted three hundred years earlier, there was little danger in the Tudor period that the liberty of the Cinque Ports would constitute a threat to the king's control of the south-east coast.

The other jurisdiction which should be mentioned in this connection is that of the Lord Admiral. The Admiralty court administered not the common law but the *Lex Maritima*, which was a blend of civil law and custom. In the early sixteenth century the Lord Admiral held jurisdiction over all matters of wreck and prize, commercial disputes, and felony or treason committed on the high seas – that is, below the low tidal mark and outside enclosed creeks and estuaries. The Admiral's authority was that of the king, and was exercised *ex officio*, without commission. It was exercised both directly, through the Admiralty court presided over by a professional judge, and indirectly through the local courts of the Vice-Admirals of the coasts.[16] These officials were local gentlemen, appointed by the Lord Admiral in the king's name, who also performed administrative and police duties within their jurisdictions. The Admiral claimed 20 per cent of the value of all lawful prizes, in addition to fines, amercements and confiscations, and the Vice-Admirals retained a proportion of these profits. A number of places also claimed exemption from the Admiral's jurisdiction, and administered the maritime law themselves for their own profit. Most of these were privileged towns, such as Great Yarmouth, or wider franchises like the Cinque Ports and the bishopric of Durham. However, there were also some individual manors, situated on the coast, which claimed similar privileges, and where the law was administered by a steward or bailiff controlling no more than a few hundred yards of foreshore. In these circumstances it is not surprising that smuggling and other evasions were relatively easy, or that piracy proved extremely difficult to control. The situation was so unsatisfactory that in 1536 piracy (which embraced any felony committed at sea) was removed from the jurisdiction of the

Admiral by statute, and placed under the common law.[17] The civil
law rules of evidence, which were used by the *Lex Maritima* made it
almost impossible to secure convictions, whereas at the common
law it was only necessary to convince the jury. Thereafter pirates
were tried by special commissions of oyer and terminer sitting in
the most convenient county, and the Lord Admiral was automa-
tically a member of every such commission. The conviction rate
was certainly improved, and Wapping became the conventional
execution place for pirates, but the problem was not brought under
control until the following century.

Outside the realm of England the Crown held various dependent
territories which were special jurisdictions in one sense or another.
Of these the most eccentric was the Isle of Man, which had been
virtually autonomous since it was conferred on the Stanley family
by King Henry IV in 1405.[18] The Stanleys styled themselves 'Kings
of Man' until 1504, when, on the death of the second Earl of Derby,
his son reverted to the earlier title of *dominus*. The island was to
remain in the possession of the Stanleys and their heirs until 1765,
when it was formally repossessed by the Crown. All the functions of
government were carried on in the name of the lord, and both the
laws and the institutions of the island were distinctive. The law was
customary and mainly of Norse origin. It had been codified in the
early fifteenth century, but was subject to amendment only by
interpretation. The authority of the English parliament was not
recognised, and there was no local provision for legislation. The
Keys, which consisted of 24 freeholders nominated by the lord, was
more in the nature of a grand jury than a miniature House of
Commons. The government of the island was vested in the lord's
council, and in the deemsters, who were magistrates resembling
Justices of the peace. Unlike the justices, however, whose commission was periodically renewed, the deemsters were appointed by the
lord for life, barring criminal misdemeanour. The high court of the
island was called the Tynwald. It was held in the name of the lord,
and convened regularly twice a year, functioning very much in the
manner of the English quarter sessions. Ecclesiastically the island
formed half of the Scottish see of Sodor and Man, which also
covered most of the Hebrides. The bishopric appears to have been
vacant for some twenty years prior to 1530, but the situation is
extremely vague because there was also an alternative English
succession from the early fifteenth century, and in 1542 the diocese

was placed by English statute under the control of York. Thereafter the succession is clear as far as Man is concerned, but the Scottish jurisdiction became first ambiguous, and then vague, and finally disappeared altogether in the seventeenth century. The reformation caused few problems that were recorded. The same bishop served undisturbed from 1546 to 1556, and the see then remained conveniently vacant until 1570.[19] Thereafter it was regularly occupied down to the present century.

Somewhat less eccentric, and a great deal more important strategically, were the Channel Islands. Originally part of Normandy, their formal separation from that province was only recognised by Henry VII in 1495. The law of the islands continued to be based upon the customs of Normandy, and French was the main language. There was, however, no yearning on the part of the islanders to return to French rule, and although there were occasional scares about 'fifth columnists', their loyalty to the English Crown was regularly commented upon. Each of the main islands, Jersey and Guernsey, was governed in the name of the king by an officer usually called the Captain, whose duties were both civil and military.[20] The magistrates were called jurats, and were appointed for life by the Captain, in consultation with the island magnates. There were twelve jurats on each island, and seven constituted the quorum necessary to hold a court. The most solemn island court was called the Chief Pleas, and resembled the English quarter sessions in function and status. Originally the English justices in Eyre had visited the islands, and the assize judges had at first followed that custom, but such visits had been discontinued in the fourteenth century, and by the Tudor period the only oversight rested with the king's Council, to whom the Captains were responsible. On Jersey and Guernsey the Chief Pleas were presided over by the island bailiff, who was the Captain's civilian deputy. Alderney was subject to the Captain of Guernsey, and its court, which was of lesser status, was presided over by the prevot. The prevot, like the bailiff, was a royal officer, but of lesser dignity. The sitation on Sark is less clear. In theory it had a court, a prevot, and jurats under the control of the Captain of Jersey, but in practice the island does not seem to have been continuously inhabited, and when it was taken briefly by the French in 1549, it was alleged that no one was living there.[21] Each Captain had a council through which he conducted the administration. Relations between the Captains and the chief island families were not always easy, but by custom the bailiff was always an island worthy, and the jurats had to be natives. Consequently the captains were unable to fill their councils with English officers and a reasonable balance was maintained. The captains were always English and normally resident, although Edward Seymour, Duke of Somerset and Lord Protector, also held both captaincies from 1546 until his death in 1552. This does not seem to have done any harm to the government of the islands, although it may explain why Sark was temporarily lost at that time.

Each of the main islands also had a body called the Estates, but this was neither elected not representative, and so did not constitute a kind of parliament. The Estates consisted of the bailiff and jurats, plus the rectors and constables of each of the island parishes. Its function was primarily consultative, but it could petition the king's Council direct if it considered that the customs and liberties of the islanders, which had been confirmed by a charter of Henry VII, were being infringed. English legislation did not apply, and the Estates had no legislative function; consequently law could only be extended or amended by judicial interpretation – as in the Isle of Man. The one respect in which the Estates did resemble the English parliament was that it had the exclusive right to grant taxation. In fact this right was rarely exercised, except for defence, and the routine expenses of government seem to have been met from regular dues, and from the profits of justice. The garrisons which were maintained on both the main islands were paid for chiefly by the English Crown. Royal commissions were occasionally issued, but never for judicial purposes. For all practical purposes the island courts were autonomous, but the equity jurisdiction of Star Chamber did apply, as an aspect of the Council's authority. Ecclesiastically the islands were subject to the Norman bishopric of Coutances. In 1496 Henry VII obtained a papal bull transferring them to the jurisdiction of Salisbury, and then in 1499 to Winchester, but nobody paid any attention. The royal supremacy and the dissolution of the religious houses were accepted without any recorded protest, and there seems to have been positive enthusiasm for Protestantism when it first appeared. However the Bishop of Coutances continued to exercise authority of a sort over the two island deans, who were appointed after 1535 by the English Crown. In 1550 it was actually confirmed that the bishop exercised his jurisdiction in the islands under the king as Supreme Head. During Mary's reign three Guernsey women were executed for heresy, more than died in the whole province of York.[22] The anomaly was finally rectified in 1568, when a dispute caused someone to look in the archives and discover the bull of 1499. The islands were then formally and finally declared to be part of the diocese of Winchester, under whose jurisdiction they thereafter remained.

Like the Channel Islands, Calais had originally been a part of the English possessions in France. Captured by Edward III in 1347, its French population had been expelled and replaced with English colonists. It had survived the French reconquests of the fifteenth century, and was regarded as the key to English control of the Narrow Seas. The author of the 'Libel of English Policy' in the 1430s had described Calais and Dover as the 'two eyes' of the king of England. At the beginning of the Tudor period the Calais Pale consisted of about 120 square miles of territory, with a sea coast eighteen miles long. The population numbered about 12,000, most of whom were in the town itself, although there were villages attached to the secondary fortresses of Guisnes, Hammes and Newnhambridge.[23] Unlike the Channel Islands, both the language and the law of Calais were English, and the statutes of the English parliament were binding. By 1509 the main strategic value of Calais had nothing to do with the control of the seas; rather it was a bridgehead for use against France whenever the king of England should feel so inclined. For that reason security was a prime consideration, and the governor, or Lord Deputy, commanded a garrison of 800–1000 men, which was constantly reinforced and kept up to strength. There were three jurisdictions within the Pale. The Lord Deputy, or a professional judge on his behalf, heard pleas of the Crown according to the common law of England. The Deputy was assisted by a council, and by four principal officers, the Marshall, who was responsible for all police work, the Treasurer and Comptroller, who between them managed the money, and the Porter, who controlled access both by land and sea. The second jurisdiction was that of the mayor and corporation of the town, who heard most routine party pleas, and managed the daily lives of the inhabitants in much the same way as their colleagues in mainland chartered boroughs. In 1536 Calais was brought into line with other such boroughs by being granted parliamentary representation. The third jurisdiction was that of the mayor and company of the Staple. The Staplers were the monopolistic fraternity who traded in raw wool, and whose head-quarters were in Calais. Originally they had been by far the richest of the English merchant companies, and one of the conditions of their monopoly was that they paid the royal garrison in Calais. By Henry VIII's reign their trade was in full decline and these payments were a burden which they could scarcely sustain. The Staplers court heard all pleas relating to their own members or their own business, and demarcation disputes with the town were naturally frequent. The Lord Deputy was also the military com-mander, generally responsible for security and for the discipline of the garrison. Ecclesiastically Calais was an archiepiscopal peculiar of Canterbury, and this may help to explain why protestant ideas took root in the town so early, and caused so much trouble to Lord Lisle when he was Deputy in the 1530s. Under Mary the heresy of the citizens was believed to have been one of the causes why the town was betrayed to the French in January 1558.[24] There is very little evidence to support such a hypothesis, and the true reason for the disaster seems to have lain in a combination of penny pinching and military complacency. By the time of its fall Calais was costing over £20,000 a year to defend, which was well beyond the capacity of the Merchant Staplers, and a good case could be made for saying that it was not worth it. Elizabeth made strenuous but unsuccessful efforts to recover the town between 1559 and 1565, and its loss was one of the factors which helped to direct English policy into new channels by the end of the century.

By far the largest of the overseas dependencies of the English Crown was the Lordship of Ireland, elevated into a kingdom in 1541 by Henry VIII, and confirmed in that status by the pope in 1555. In theory the whole of Ireland was subject to English rule, but in practice that had never been the case. By 1490 the English position had recovered somewhat from the low point which it had reached thirty years earlier, but there were still three main divisions of Ireland, reflecting the effectiveness of royal authority.[25] The Pale, that is, the region surrounding and to the south of Dublin, was ruled as fully as most parts of England. The so-called 'obedient lands', the Anglo-Irish lordships which occupied most of south and south-eastern Ireland, were under a looser control, determined by the power and attitudes of the local magnates. 'Wild' Ireland, comprising most of the north and west, consisted of Gaelic tribal territory where the king's writ did not run, and where his authority was only occasionally recognised to suit the convenience of the chieftains. The Pale was shired in the English manner, each county being divided into 'baronies', which were the equivalent of hundreds. The 'obedient lands' consisted partly of shires and partly of franchises, rather similar in their nature to those in the marches of Wales, except that none of them were in the king's hands. The sheriff in each county conducted his court twice a year, dealing mainly with misdemeanours, while the county courts handled party issues, as had originally been the case in England. There were no quarter sessions, because there were no commissions of the peace, but major offences were usually referred to special judicial commissions of oyer and terminer. These were *ad hoc* rather than regular, but were issued far more frequently than was the case on the mainland, because they had to take the place of both the assizes and the graver jurisdiction of the justices of the peace. Important cases could be, and occasionally were, referred to the central courts of King's Bench and Common Bench, which were held in Dublin as their counterparts were held in Westminster, but the inconveniencies of travel and the frequency of commissions made that an uncommon procedure.[26] The law administered was English common law in the Pale, and in the shires of the 'obedient lands'. In the franchises it was a mixture of common law and local custom. Neither the judicial system nor the common law extended to the Gaelic lands, where customary codes were enforced by the traditional tribal courts, without reference to any outside jurisdiction. Wherever the king's writ ran, it ran in the name of the Lord, or King of Ireland, and executive Acts were sealed the Great Seal of that land.

The story of the government of Ireland in the Tudor period falls neatly into two parts, divided by a major change of strategy in 1534.[27] Henry VII was primarily concerned to establish some effective control over those who governed in his name, which meant principally Gerald FitzGerald, 8th Earl of Kildare. Henry appointed first his uncle the Duke of Bedford and then his infant son the Duke of York as Lieutenants of Ireland, but both were figureheads. Real authority rested with Kildare, who was Deputy from 1479 to 1492, and again from 1496 to 1509. This reflected the policy which Henry took over from the Yorkists, of ruling through the most powerful magnate on the spot. This had been Edward's policy in England too, but as we have seen, Henry did not adopt it nearer home, except perhaps in the far north. In Ireland there was no sensible alternative to recognising the virtual autonomy of the Anglo-Irish magnates, and Henry concentrated on establishing the limited principle that they were, in the last analysis, answerable to him and to his Council in England. After making a serious mistake over Lambert Simnel, and narrowly avoiding a similar error over Perkin Warbeck, Kildare accepted that the king's authority was secure. Once Henry had established his ascendancy in principle, he was content to allow things to continue very much as before, lacking the resources to intervene more directly. He did, however, take the additional precaution in 1494 of ensuring that the Irish parliament could only be convened by his own personal command, and could deal only with matters which had been sanctioned by the English Council.[28] At the same time the vice-regal powers of the Lord Deputy were also somewhat curtailed. He could no longer on his own authority pardon treasons, or alienate any part of the royal demesne. If he needed to be absent from his post for any length of time, a locum could only be appointed with the king's express permission. Nevertheless it continued to be true that Kildare governed Ireland through a contract with the king which entitled him to retain a large share of the profits and patronage of office in return for his services. This situation continued substantially unchanged under Henry VIII. Apart from a few months in 1515, Kildare continued in office until March 1520, and his son the 9th Earl was also Lord Deputy from 1524 to 1528. After Wolsey's fall, however, the king began a series of moves which were aimed at increasing his direct control. Kildare was detained in England and the Duke of Richmond appointed Lieutenant. The Chief Justice, Patrick Bermingham, was created Deputy, and a new and predominantly English council named to assist him. The experiment was short-lived, probably because Henry's concentration span for such matters was too short. In 1530 Kildare returned to Ireland as Deputy with the English soldier Sir William Skeffington as his assistant. The Deputy's brief at this point was extremely conservative, amounting to little more than maintaining the status quo within the Anglo-Irish community, and seeking to pacify those of the Gaelic chieftains who were too close for comfort.[29]

Unfortunately the conditions for success were not present. In 1531 the Irish parliament refused a request for a subsidy, and the feuds which had rumbled for generations among the Anglo-Irish nobility, particularly the FitzGeralds and the Butlers, reached a new pitch of intensity. Kildare fell out disastrously with Skeffington, and the king began to become suspicious of his loyalty. In September 1533 the Lord Deputy was summoned to the Council to give an account of his stewardship, along with other Irish officials, but declined to come on the grounds of ill health. He also ignored warnings from the king about transferring royal ordnance from Dublin Castle to his own strongholds. By this time events in Ireland were becoming entangled with the king's Great Matter, and opponents of the Boleyn party were looking to Kildare to lead Ireland in defying Henry's authority. The Deputy, however, was not so much interested in matters of high policy as in preserving the ascendancy of his family. At the end of 1533 he was persuaded to come to England by being allowed to name his son, Lord Offaly, to act as locum in his absence. If he was expecting to take advantage of Henry's other difficulties to secure a favourable deal for himself in Ireland, then he was disappointed. After examination before the Council for his 'manifold enormities' in office, he was detained in London. Learning of his father's situation, in June 1534 Lord Offaly resigned his office, denounced the king as a heretic and renounced his allegiance.[30] Henry was unprepared for such dramatic defiance, and initially attempted to parley with 'Silken Thomas' as he was known. Encouraged by this apparent sign of weakness, Offaly began to behave as though he intended to drive the English out of Ireland altogether, and he began to recruit support among the Gaelic chieftains. Probably his real intention, like that of the Pilgrims two years later, was to force the king into a change of policy, which in his case would have guaranteed the unchallenged ascendancy of the FitzGeralds for the foreseeable future. Like the Pilgrims also, he underestimated Henry's resolution, and took his negotiating ploys too seriously. In October 1534 Skeffington returned at the head of an army of over 2,000 men – a great force by Irish standards – and the stakes were suddenly and dramatically raised. The Pale gentry, who had thought that they were taking part in a demonstration, now found themselves caught between a royal army and the increasingly Irish rhetoric of Offaly and his affinity. They had no real desire to fight against the king, and most of them hastened to submit. Meanwhile the Earl of Kildare had died in England, and Silken Thomas succeeded as the

10th Earl. Skeffington stormed his castle at Maynooth in March 1535, and Kildare took refuge among the Gaelic tribes, turning his rebellion perforce into something which looked and sounded like an Irish war of independence. Skeffington lacked the resources to go after him, but on the other hand the Gaelic tribes lacked both the will and the stamina to fight a prolonged war. In August 1535 the earl decided to gamble upon his indispensability to any future government in Ireland, and surrendered.

He miscalculated just as seriously as Robert Aske was to do. If he had been dealing only with the king and the Duke of Norfolk, that might not have been the case, but Thomas Cromwell was an altogether tougher proposition. Cromwell was prepared to sacrifice the easy (and cheap) option of pardoning Kildare and eventually returning him to office. In February 1537 the earl and his five uncles were tried for high treason and executed. Thereafter Ireland was to be governed by an English Deputy, supported by a substantial garrison. This was not just to prevent it from becoming a FitzGerald franchise, it was also to facilitate the imposition of the royal supremacy, and to avoid any repetition of the embarrassing rebuff inflicted by the parliament of 1531. Such tightening of control from London was very much in line with Cromwell's policy in the north of England and in the marches of Wales, and it did not require any constitutional changes. It did, however, require the consistent allocation of resources, and that was not always achieved. The Anglo-Irish population as a whole was perfectly amenable to this style of government, and the Irish Reformation Parliament, which met from 1535 to 1537, enacted the legislation of its English predecessor without protest. The Anglo-Irish gentry, like their English counterparts, did well out of the dissolution of the religious houses, and loyalty to Rome was not conspicuous in any part of the country. There was, however, another drawback, in addition to expense. The Anglo-Irish magnates had always had a foot in Gaelic Ireland as well. They were respected there, and recognised in its power structures. This did not prevent conflict because the Irish tribes were always at odds with each other, and the Earls of Desmond, Ormond and Kildare were regularly involved in such feuds. It did, however, mean that they knew how to deal with the Irishry, and there was little which could be described as racial or ideological strife as long as they retained their ascendancy. English deputies, on the other hand, particularly military men like Lord Leonard Grey, had no understanding of, or sympathy with, the 'wild' Irish, whom they regarded as savages. Consequently the dismantling of Anglo-Irish autonomy which followed the collapse of Silken Thomas's revolt resulted, over the following twenty years, in a steady deterioration of relations between the government in Dublin and the Gaelic chieftains.[31]

This deterioration was accelerated, but not caused, by the advent of Protestantism in England. Ecclesiastically Ireland had never been dependent upon Canterbury or York. It consisted of the four provinces of Armagh, Tuam, Dublin and Cashel, and thirty dioceses. Neither the dioceses nor the provinces corresponded with the divisions between English and Gaelic Ireland, although Dublin was mainly in the former, and Armagh and Tuam predominantly in the latter. Most of the religious houses in Dublin went down, most of those in Armagh survived, while Tuam and Cashel were about equally divided. Not even the warmest defenders of Irish Christianity have tried to claim that the late medieval Church was in good condition. Outside the Pale, and a few English towns such as Cork and Waterford, discipline was poor, and in the Gaelic lands clergy and even abbots were regularly married men with children and strong tribal loyalties. There was little appetite for reform in any of its main European guises, and the spiritual traditions of the Celtic Church were chiefly maintained by the friars, whose lack of territoriality and jurisdiction suited them to the anarchic state of Irish politics. Henry became Supreme Head of the Church in Ireland by the legislation of 1537, but apart from the disappearance of the somewhat discredited monasteries, this made little visible difference. The men of the new learning, who rallied around Cromwell in England in the late 1530s, were almost entirely absent from Ireland. The erection of the Lordship of Ireland into a kingdom in 1541 was directly related to this jurisdictional change. According to the preamble of the relevant Irish statute, 'the Irishmen and inhabitants within this realm of Ireland have not been so obedient to the king's highness. . .as they of right and according to their allegiance and bounden duties ought to have been',[32] because it was generally believed among the Irish that the temporal sovereignty of the country belonged to the pope, under whom the king held the lordship. By breaking with the pope, and

converting Ireland into a kingdom immediately after, Henry was signifying that he claimed full authority, both spiritual and temporal.
When he died in January 1547 the prospects for success looked reasonably good. Sir Anthony St Leger, who had been Deputy since 1540, had adopted a deliberately conciliatory policy towards the Irish chieftains, not with a view to restoring the pre-1534 situation, but in an attempt to incorporate them into the government on equal terms with the Anglo-Irish, a programme which had never been contemplated by Kildare and his predecessors, and which was given additional credibility by the adoption of the royal style. In response to his invitations the chieftains of FitzPatrick, O'Reilly, O'Connor, Burke of Clanrickard, MacMurrough, O'More, O'Carroll and O'Neill either came in person to the parliament or sent proctors – an altogether unprecedented situation. With the same objective in mind, St Leger also began to pursue a policy of surrender and regrant, whereby the chieftains were encouraged to surrender their tribal lands to the king, and receive them back as fiefs protected by English law. This had the great advantage, from the chieftains' point of view, of converting what had originally been communal lands into family patrimonies which could be handed on to their heirs without running the hazards of tribal custom. The deal often included a baronial title on the English model. The initial take-up rate was encouraging, and had this policy been pursued consistently and with energy over a number of years, most of the subsequent troubles of Ireland could probably have been avoided. Henry was not convinced of the merits of his Deputy's policy. He had consented to it during a lapse of concentration, tried to repudiate it, and ended by giving it a grudging endorsement. His reluctance was perhaps due to the fact that the idea had originated in Ireland and not in England. Towards the end of his reign and contrary to custom, Henry raised troops in Ireland for service in Scotland and in France. This created many difficulties for his officials, but it did have the incidental effect of putting Ireland on a par with England in supporting the king's war. It also removed a number of troublesome elements from Irish society, a technique which the English muster commissioners had learned some time earlier.
    Without a committed body of Irish Protestant support, however small, the imposition of the Edwardian Reformation became

exclusively a function of English power. The 'Book of Reformation' of November 1548 was issued by the English Council, and enforced by the Lord Deputy without a shadow of consent.[33] Similarly the Prayer Book of 1549 was introduced on the authority of the English statute, without having been approved by the Irish parliament. Given their commitment to vernacular worship, the reformers should immediately have turned their attention to the production of a Gaelic Prayer Book. That did not happen because none of them were Gaelic speakers. A Latin version was produced, and Gaelic sermons and prayers were accepted, but the new rite found little acceptance outside the Pale, and little enthusiasm inside. John Bale, the ultra-Protestant Bishop of Ossory, believed that his vigorous campaign in 1552 and 1553 had enjoyed considerable success. He probably deceived himself, because within a few months of Mary's accession and well before it happened in England, the whole Edwardian Reformation was swept away. Had Mary lived longer, the political wounds inflicted by Bale and his kind might well have healed, but Elizabeth was committed to her brother's settlement rather than her father's, and Protestant-ism again became the religion of the English ascendancy. She did not make Somerset's mistake, and carefully waited for the Irish parliament to pass its Acts of Supremacy and Uniformity in 1560 before embarking upon a policy of enforcement. Nor was that policy, when it came, particularly rigorous, but it was accompanied by a new and more aggressive secular policy, for which it appeared to supply a justifying ideology.

That policy originated in Somerset's impatience with the slow dividends of St Leger's attempts at assimilation. For every two steps forward there had been one back, and in the summer of 1546 there had been a serious Gaelic intrusion into Offaly. In March 1547, as a direct consequence, the English Privy Council decided to estab-lish English garrisons in the tribal lands adjoining the Pale, in order to protect it from this type of depredation. A smouldering war resulted, which compelled the Deputy to establish military control over the whole midland area. That had been accomplished by the spring of 1549, but the resulting situation was unstable, and it was decided to establish English civilian settlements around the garri-sons. This immediately aroused fears of large-scale expropriations among the Irish chieftains, and the security situation became worse rather than better. However Leix-Offaly, the area bordering the

Pale immediately to the west of Kildare, was successfully planted with English freeholders in 1556, and shired as King's County and Queen's County in 1557. In spite of the abrupt change in the religious climate in 1553, there was considerable continuity of secular policy. West Meath, to the north of Offaly, had already been shired without plantation in 1542, during St Leger's conciliatory regime, but the counties created in 1557 were the result of military control, rather than lack of opposition. By 1552 Edward's Council was reconsidering its forward policy in Ireland because of the cost, and was beginning to experiment with the rehabilitation of the Anglo-Irish magnates. Gerald FitzGerald, the heir to the Earldom of Kildare, was restored in blood in 1552, but no further progress was made before the king's death. Mary reinstated St Leger as Deputy in November 1553, and restored the Earldom of Kildare in 1554, but she also pressed ahead with the plantation of Leix-Offaly, her Council apparently regarding that as a particular solution to a particular problem rather than any kind of blueprint for future strategy.[34] St Leger and Kildare were soon at odds, and the former was recalled at the beginning of 1556. However there was no intention of returning to the pre-1534 situation, and the appointment of Thomas Radcliffe, Lord FitzWalter and soon to be Earl of Sussex, as Lord Deputy in April 1556 signalled a change of direction which was to be general and permanent.

The policy of Sussex and his successors, with the backing of Elizabeth's Council, built on the precedent of the Leix-Offaly plantation. Between 1560 and 1585 the whole of Gaelic Ireland was shired. English law, English courts and English religion were officially introduced. Irish resistance was frequently violent, but until the 1590s, sporadic and uncoordinated, as was natural from a politically fragmented society. There were further plantations in Down in 1570, Antrim in 1572–3 and Munster in 1584. Anglo-Irish reaction was divided. Some of the 'old English' of the Pale adopted Protestantism and supported the government; others felt far more alienated from the 'new English' than they did from the Irish, and maintained their Catholic loyalties, but seldom became involved in overt opposition. The Irish parliament represented the English ascendancy, and English gentlemen and courtiers were given extensive grants of Irish lands. This did not amount to wholesale expropriation, and was not the result of a deliberate policy to dispossess the Irish landholders. Resistance to government policy resulted in confiscation, and confiscated lands were divided between the loyal Irish and the English. In theory the distinction between the 'obedient lands' and the Irishry disappeared, and the whole country became one kingdom governed on the English model, although the commission of the peace was conspicuous by its absence. Resident judicial commissioners had occasionally been appointed from the 1490s to support the sheriff's jurisdiction in areas where access to the central courts was particularly inconvenient, such as Kilkenny and Waterford, and where occasional commissions were also deemed to be inadequate. During the reign of Elizabeth this provision was adapted and expanded by the creation of provincial councils on the model of the Council of the North.[35] One such was established for Connaught in 1569, and another for Munster in 1571. Nevertheless, practice corresponded only roughly with theory, and military activity was constantly required in one part of Ireland or another to maintain a semblance of the queen's peace. Attempts to establish Protestantism were peculiarly ineffective, and the native population, at all social levels, remained loyal not merely to the old ways but also to the papacy, which they had by then rediscovered. Catholic spirituality was a great deal stronger in Ireland in 1600 than it had been in 1550, thanks partly to dislike of the English ascendancy and partly to the activities of Catholic missionaries and agents anxious to use the country as a base for operations against England.

It was one thing, however, to resent English domination, and another to do anything about it. The few hundred English troops normally stationed in the Pale, competently led and adequately equipped, repeatedly demonstrated their ability to cope with sporadic risings, or the occasional incursions of the Scots into Antrim. However even the prospect of foreign support could destabilise this situation. When James FitzMaurice landed with a mere handful of Spanish and Italian troops under a papal banner at Smerwick in 1579 he dislodged a stone which triggered several revolts, and the Lord Deputy, Sir William Drury, quickly discovered that he could not trust the Anglo-Irish peers who were supposed to be backing him. However trivial the occasion, by early 1580 it was clear to the English Council that they confronted a serious problem. Drury was replaced by Lord Grey of Wilton, and an army numbering over 6,000 men was sent to support him. The risings were suppressed in a matter of weeks, and the garrison at

Smerwick was massacred on the grounds that the pope was not a recognised belligerent. Nevertheless the lessons of deep-seated discontent and uncertain loyalty were not learned, and in 1593 Hugh O'Neill, the 2nd Earl of Tyrone, demonstrated conclusively how limited the Elizabethan achievement in Ireland had really been. A man with a powerful hereditary position, and endowed with both skill and charisma, he was able to wage a war upon the English government which lasted for nine years, costing hundreds of thousands of pounds, as well as innumerable lives and reputations.[36] In the context of the Anglo- Spanish war Tyrone's rebellion was really dangerous, as the large-scale Spanish landing at Kinsale in 1601 made clear. His eventual defeat consolidated the English hold upon Ireland, but it had become a colonial government, holding down a reluctant and occasionally rebellious country. In this respect it was quite unlike any of the other non-English possessions of the Tudor Crown. In Wales, the Channel Islands, and even the Isle of Man, Elizabeth's authority was acknowledged without challenge, Protestantism was the majority religion, and the local elites were thoroughly incorporated into a system of government which endorsed a large measure of central control. By contrast, what remained of the Irish elite was very uncertain in its temporal allegiance, and religiously alienated. The new English elite was loyal, and Protestant, but had no natural following outside the English plantations, and its vulnerability was to be conclusively demonstrated in 1641. Of all the areas of special jurisdiction, Ireland was the most turbulent and least successful. Whether the situation would have been better if Cromwell and Burghley had refrained from interfering is hard to say. Elizabeth did not feel that she could tolerate the existence of an independent Irishry in the way that her father had done, and in the changed circumstances of the late sixteenth century, she was probably right. However the real failure of Tudor government in Ireland was that it did not succeed in convincing the Gaelic elite that its interests would be better served by consistent cooperation than by unpredictable bouts of disaffection.

Notes

1. G. Dyfnallt Owen, *Elizabethan Wales* (Cardiff, 1964), citing PRO Wales 4 Gaol Files, Denbigh 10/4.

2. R. A. Griffiths, *Rhys ap Thomas and his Family* (1994).
3. G. R. Elton, *The Tudor Constitution*, 2nd edn (1982) p.202.
4. Statute 26 Henry VIII c. 6; *Statutes of the Realm*, vol. III, pp. 500–3.
5. Owen, *Elizabethan Wales*, pp. 169–97.
6. 34 & 35 Henry VIII c. 26; *Statutes of the Realm*, vol. III, p. 926.
7. J. Youings, 'The Council of the West', *Transactions of the Royal Historical Society*, 5th series, 10 (1960) pp. 40ff.
8. BL Harleian MS 433, f. 264v.
9. G. R. Elton, 'Politics and the Pilgrimage of Grace', in *Studies in Tudor and Stuart Politics and Government*, vol. III (1983) pp. 183–215.
10. F. W. Brooks, *The Council of the North* (1953), pp. 16ff. *State Papers of Henry VIII* (1832–52) vol. V, pp. 402–11.
11. Sir Thomas Percy had been restored to the earldom of Northumberland by Mary in 1557. See R. Reid, 'The rebellion of the Earls, 1569', *Transactions of the Royal Historical Society*, new series, 20 (1906) pp. 171ff.
12. M. James, *Family, Lineage and Civil Society* (Oxford, 1974) p. 48.
13. R. Somerville, 'The Duchy of Lancaster Council and the Court of Duchy Chamber', *Transactions of the Royal Historical Society*, 4th series, 23, (1941) pp. 159ff.
14. A. L. Rowse, *Tudor Cornwall* (1941) pp. 65–6.
15. F. W. Brooks, 'The Cinque Ports', *Mariners Mirror*, 15 (1929) pp. 142–91.
16. R. G. Marsden, 'The Vice Admirals of the Coasts', *English Historical Review*, 22 (1907).
17. 28 Henry VIII c. 15; *Statutes of the Realm*, vol. III, pp. 671–2.
18. R. H. Kinvig, *History of the Isle of Man* (Oxford, 1944) p. 123.
19. *Handbook of British Chronology*, (1985) pp. 315, 273.
20. A. J. Eaglestone, *The Channel Islands under Tudor Government* (Cambridge, 1949).
21. Ibid.
22. J. Foxe, *Acts and Monuments of the English Martyrs*, eds S. R. Cattley and George Townshend (1837–41) vol. VIII, pp. 226–8.
23. C. G. Cruickshank, *Army Royal: An Account of Henry VIII's Invasion of France* (1969) pp. 19–24; P. Morgan, 'The Government of Calais, 1485–1558' (D.Phil. Thesis, Oxford, 1967).
24. Sir Edward Carne (in Rome) wrote to the queen at the end of January to report the currency of that version of the story there. A report sent to Spain at the same time said 'The governor of Calais was a great heretic, like all those who were with him there' *Calendar of State Papers, Spanish*, vol. XIII (1954) pp. 346–7.
25. S. G. Ellis, *Reform and Revival: English Government in Ireland, 1470–1534* (1986).
26. S. G. Ellis, *Tudor Ireland*, (1985) pp. 151–82.
27. S. G. Ellis, 'Tudor Policy and the Kildare Ascendancy in the Lordship of Ireland, 1496- 1534', *Irish Historical Studies*, 20 (1977) pp. 807–30; B. Bradshaw, *The Irish Constitutional Revolution of the Sixteenth Century* (1979).
28. Ellis, *Tudor Ireland*, pp. 163–4.
29. Ibid., pp. 119–20.

30. Ibid., pp. 124–5.
31. Bradshaw, *Irish Constitutional Revolution*, pp. 174–80.
32. *The Statutes at Large passed in the Parliaments held in Ireland* (1786–1801) vol. I, pp. 176–7.
33. B. Bradshaw, 'The Edwardian Reformation in Ireland', *Archivum Hibernicum*, 24 (1976–7).
34. Ellis, *Tudor Ireland*, p. 233.
35. N. Canny, *The Elizabethan Conquest of Ireland: A Pattern Established, 1565–1576* (1976) 5; L. Irwin, 'The Irish Presidency Courts, 1569–1672', *The Irish Jurist*, new series, 12 (1977).
36. Ellis, *Tudor Ireland*, pp. 298–311. C. Falls, *Elizabeth's Irish Wars* (1950). J.J. Silke, *Kinsale* (1970).

8 Regional and Provincial Identity

It is very tempting to ascribe the Tudor failure in Ireland to cultural factors – differences of law, religion, language and social structure. However, such an interpretation would be based upon nineteenth- or twentieth-century conceptions of national identity. Religious difference followed political alienation rather than preceding it, and there is very little evidence before the seventeenth century that the Irish saw themselves as being in any sense one people. Wales shared most of the cultural characteristics of Ireland. In both countries native law was abrogated, and the customary courts relegated to fringe activities. English was the official language of both law and government, and tribal customs of dress and behaviour were severely discouraged. But in Wales Tudor government worked. Culturally the Channel Islands were part of Normandy, and yet no subjects of the English Crown were more loyal. If English overlordship was resented in any of these territories, it was not for differences of language or manners, but for much more tangible considerations of land and office. Both Wales and the Channel Islands were run, in the ordinary day-by-day sense, by their own elites. The fact that the Earl of Leicester held great estates in North Wales, or that the Captain of Jersey was an Englishman, mattered much less than the authority of the jurats or the justices of the peace, who mediated royal government to the people. In Ireland it was the plantations and the granting of large estates to English gentlemen which created the fear of expropriation, and gave English rule the face of a colonial and military tyranny. The Welsh gentry became largely anglicised in their own interest, but that did not destroy either their identity or their authority. It is therefore necessary to be extremely cautious in attributing political consequences to cultural causes, or at least to cultural causes as we would normally perceive them.

A dislike of outside interference in the affairs of closely knit communities was almost universal, and played a part in all the major disturbances of the Tudor period. In 1497 the Cornishmen were not interested in Perkin Warbeck, but deeply resented the king's attempts to levy a general tax to help pay for the defence of the northern borders against the Scots.

> They muttered extremely that it was a thing not to be suffered that for a littel stir of the Scots, soon blown over, they should be thus grinded to powder with payments: and said it was for those to pay who had too much and lived idly. But they would eat their bread that they got with the sweat of their brows, and no man should take it from them.[11]

It was not so much that they felt themselves to be different from the rest of the king's subjects, but that they could not conceive of any political entity as large as the realm of England, or believe that they had any responsibility to it. The idea that it was 'a different world beyond the Tamar' is even more appealing as an explanation of what happened in 1549, when the rebels listed among their grievances the fact that many Cornishmen spoke no English, and therefore rejected the new Prayer Book as being 'like a Christmas game'.[2] The Cornish language had been in decline for some time by the mid-sixteenth century, and although there may well have been fishing communities in the far south-west where English was not understood, that was not the position of the majority of Cornishmen, and particularly not of the citizens of Bodmin, where the rebellion had its origins. As Archbishop Cranmer pointed out, there was little logic in rejecting a liturgy in one unfamiliar language in favour of another (Latin) which was even less widely understood. The rising of 1549 was probably less religious in its motivation than it was made to appear, because the articles were drawn up by the conservative clergy, who played a prominent part in its leadership. As far as the Cornish were concerned, it was the introduction of change by outside authority which was unacceptable, rather than the nature of that change. They were also encouraged by the self-induced belief that these changes were the work of 'evil councillors', and did not correspond with the true wishes of the king, a view which the circumstances of a minority made particularly appealing.

If cultural distinctiveness as we now understand it was a major factor in Tudor rebellions, then it becomes extremely difficult to understand why there should have been great revolts in Yorkshire,

Lincolnshire, Devon, Oxfordshire, Norfolk and Kent, but not in Wales. Wales had cultural leadership of a sort in the persons of its bards, a dwindling group of professional poets, who were fiercely critical of the anglicising influences which were slowly depriving them of their patrons and their audiences. However the bards were not political agitators.[3] Paradoxically, this was partly the result of their own conservatism, because they were following an ancient tradition and prophecy when they hailed Henry Tudor, who bore a Welsh name and was partly Welsh by descent, as the long-awaited messiah of the Welsh nation – the *mab darogon*.[4] It is very doubtful whether Henry understood a word of Welsh, and he was a big disappointment to the followers of bardic prophecy, but they never entirely lost faith in the Tudors, and never sought to use their influence against them. At the same time Wales also developed a cultural leadership of a more contemporary nature, in the form of scholars such as Sir John Price and William Salesbury. Both were Renaissance scholars educated, perforce, outside Wales, which had no university, but believing strongly in the importance of their own vernacular. Price was a pioneer of Welsh language publishing, and essayed a translation of the 1549 Prayer Book, which seems to have enjoyed little currency. Salesbury was more successful with a hastily prepared version of the gospels and epistles, the *Cynnifer Llith a Ban*, which appeared in 1551.[5] The bards, unsurprisingly, were hostile to the reformation and contemptuous of its introduction in the reign of Edward VI, but the scholars were divided, and there were from the first some Welsh-speaking clergy who embraced the new doctrine. Thanks to the leadership of such men as Salesbury and Richard Davies, both the Prayer Book and the New Testament had been translated by 1567, and the whole Bible by 1588.

The attitude of Tudor governments towards the Welsh language did not conform to any modern notions of logic. Having excluded the vernacular from all official business, the Council and parliament were fully supportive of the religious translation programme. Theoretically Welsh could not be used in a court of law, but in practice litigants very often pleaded in the vernacular, which was then translated for the benefit of the records. Welsh grammar schools made not the slightest attempt to impose the use of English. The language of education by the Elizabethan period was good humanist Latin, and it was said of John Williams, later Bishop of Lincoln and Archbishop of York, that when he went from Ruthin

School to St John's College, Cambridge in 1598 he spoke good Latin and Welsh, but very little English.[6] The Welsh gentry learned English because it was the qualification for office, and because it created wider social and economic opportunities. The English might make pejorative remarks about Welsh poverty and kleptomania, but the Welsh were not oversensitive to such jibes when careers at court or in the Church were on offer. Welsh became the language of worship, not at the expense of English, but at the expense of Latin, and whereas it had been very rare in the late medieval period for Welsh bishops either to speak the language or to reside on their cures, for a century after 1558 they did both. Nor were the Welsh naturally given to recusancy. The religious instincts of ordinary people were intensely conservative, and seminary trained Catholic clergy like Huw Owen were as disconcerted as their protestant rivals by the unenlightened state of popular piety.[7] The distinctive culture of Wales was not an issue, and created no barriers between the Welsh elite and their English neighbours. The Welsh-speaking areas had never been a single, independent political entity, and bardic nostalgia was for something which, in important ways, had never been. At the same time Tudor dynastic propaganda, and the need to give British Christianity a non-papal origin, created an intellectual fashion for the 'matter of Britain'. Archbishop Matthew Parker became intensely interested in Celtic saints and bishops, and King Arthur, who had won his battles against the Saxons, was reinvented as a culture hero for a new, and predominantly English, patriotism. Shakespeare's Frenchmen and Spaniards might be spineless or ridiculous, but Captain Fluellen, for all his eccentricity, was a valiant and careful soldier.

The English language itself had evolved rapidly during the fifteenth century, and continued to change, although rather less rapidly, throughout the sixteenth. The Lollard Bible, which had been translated at the end of the fourteenth century, was almost as archaic and incomprehensible to the subjects of Henry VIII as it is to us. The written language had also become standardised, and although the Book of Common Prayer was widely unpopular in conservative areas, no one from a place where English was normally spoken complained that they could not understand it. Written Scots, which was an English dialect, looks outlandish to anyone mainly familiar with Renaissance English, but it is, and was, perfectly comprehensible. How far a countryman from the fringes of Exmoor would have understood the speech of a man from Redesdale or Norfolk may be doubted, but those who travelled and needed to speak to each other – merchants, students and gentlemen on business – never had any serious difficulty making themselves understood. The English language, like the common law, was a unifying force, and became more so once it was adopted for liturgical purposes. Latin had been equally universal but since it could be understood only by the educated, that had not been particularly significant. There had been five different Latin rites used in different parts of England and Wales, but the Book of Common Prayer was everywhere the same. Theoretically a traveller could have walked into matins in any parish Church in England, and found the same prayers being said, and the same portions of scripture read. It was probably never quite as simple as that in practice, but uniformity was an ideal taken very seriously by the Elizabethan Church. The clergy used Latin, and the aristocracy used French, when corresponding with their continental friends, but English was the first language of all classes from Southampton to Berwick and from Shropshire to Norfolk. It was the language alike of government, business and religion, and since it was spoken nowhere else in Europe, it created a sense of distinctiveness as well as unity.

In so far as there were cultural differences between different parts of England, they were mainly social and economic in their nature. Strong traditional loyalties made some areas slow to change, and hard to govern from a distance. It was said that the northern border clans, such as the Robsons and the Fenwicks, recognised no virtues in a man save courage in battle and loyalty to his lord. The society portrayed in the border ballads of the previous century appears to have been of that kind, brutal and amoral by the standards both of the Church and of normal lowland society. Northern society in general was more traditional in its loyalties than that of the Midlands or the south, and expected its leaders to observe a code of conduct which was not necessarily consistent with their obligations to the Tudor state.[8] The Pilgrimage of Grace was a rag-bag of a movement, which had been preceded by intrigues and conspiracies involving a number of courtiers and regional noblemen. However the initiative for action, when it came, came mostly from the commons, who revealed their innate conservatism by moving immediately to involve their natural leaders, the local gentry. Most of these men later tried to excuse their actions on the ground that they had been coerced, but there was little sign of that at the time. They acted as they considered their status and its attendant responsibilities obliged them to. By embracing innovative policies, the king was betraying his trust, and a gentleman's honour required him to resist change when it adversely affected the interests of his dependants – and even more if it adversely affected his own. Lord Darcy, already an old man at the time of the rising, declared that Henry had dishonoured himself in listening to the advice of such upstarts as Cromwell and Cranmer, and that he, Darcy, would be dishonoured in his own eyes if he did not protest to the best of his ability. Whether this sort of reaction could be ascribed to a sense of regional identity seems to be highly doubtful, but it was certainly an area where such conservative views were prevalent. The attempt to restore dissolved religious houses, which was another feature of the rising, arose partly from a similar conservatism, partly from the social usefulness of such houses in remote areas, and partly from a desire to protect the rights of patrons. No generalisation is entirely valid, but many people, probably a majority at each social level, considered that the traditional loyalties which were embodied in their way of life were more valid, and more binding, than their allegiance to the king. Since, however, they were not prepared to fight the king to protect that way of life, it continued to be eroded by the pressures of the state.

Between 1530 and 1580 those same pressures converted England into a protestant country, and added the reformed faith to the sense of national identity which was already emerging. By the time of the Armada in 1588 it was almost as necessary as loyalty to the Crown, and more necessary than English speech. This left the Catholic recusants as an alienated and potentially subversive minority. There was little that they could do about it, because the papal bull *Regnans in Excelsis* of 1570 had explicitly deposed Elizabeth and released her subjects from their allegiance. It was therefore impossible to accept papal authority and remain a loyal subject. Life is not logical, and the great majority of English Catholics, whatever William Allen may have said to the contrary, were prepared to die for their country against Spain. However, the government can hardly be blamed for not accepting professions to that effect at their face value. There were recusants in most English and Welsh counties, but their numbers, and consequently the threat which they presented, varied greatly from one region to another. In Norfolk or Kent recusant gentlemen could be identified and contained with relative ease, but in Lancashire or Durham it was a different story. The Durham Catholics had already risen in 1569 without success, and defeat at that time had made the threat notional twenty years later. Lancashire, however, was a 'Catholic county' where the majority of the gentry practised the old faith, and many others, even of the justices, were sympathetic.[9] Logically Lancashire should have had a sense of identity which set it apart, and should have presented a serious threat of subversion, or even rebellion, during the war with Spain. Such, however, was not the case. That was partly because conservative loyalties worked against each other, and the traditional authority of the Stanleys was exercised on the Crown's behalf; but it was also because the ties which bound the men of Lancashire to the court, and to their neighbours in other counties were, in most cases, stronger than those which bound them to remote ecclesiastical authority.

Counties may have been the principal political and administrative subdivisions of England, but there are few signs that they had, or developed, cultural identities. A nobleman or a gentleman might well refer to Worcestershire or Hampshire as his 'country', meaning that area in which he felt at home, and where he exercised some influence or authority. However, it is easy to overestimate the importance of local loyalties, just as it is tempting to overestimate the closeness of kindreds. Family ties can explain behaviour patterns, but it would be very rash to assume that kindreds always acted in harmony. Feuds among members of county families were as common as alliances. Similarly, although the counties were ancient units, they did not correspond with the great affinities of earlier centuries, much less with primitive tribal territories. A Berkshire man would not have felt himself to be different from his neighbours in Oxfordshire or Buckinghamshire to the same degree that an Englishman felt different from a Frenchman or a Scot. In the early sixteenth century a form of tribalism still lingered about the great pilgrimage shrines. The tenants of the bishopric of Durham described themselves as the men of St Cuthbert, and there were fierce debates about the relative merits of Our Lady of Pew and Our Lady of Walsingham. The Reformation did not immediately extinguish such loyalties, but they withered away under the unrelenting pressure of official Protestantism, and nothing similar took their place until the emergence of league football. Men took pride in their communities. Francis Drake and Walter Raleigh were Devonians, Nicholas Ridley was a Northumbrian; but they were Englishmen first. The sentiments which divided a Swabian from a Bavarian or a Galician from a Castilian were only weakly reflected within the Tudor state.

The hostilities which did divide Tudor England were of a different kind. The bitter quarrels which took place between religious reformers and conservatives reflected no divisions of social status, and no existing communities. Towns and families were torn apart, and neighbour set against neighbour. There was no religious war in England because the government retained control, but there was persecution of dissenters, and outbreaks of communal violence, until the long reign of Elizabeth gave England's distinctive Protestantism an unchallengeable ascendancy. However the largest-scale violence, and the most widespread, was only partly religious in its inspiration. The 'camping summer' of 1549 was caused mainly by social and economic grievances, and its psychological impact was out of all proportion to the real political danger which it represented. Right across the Midlands and the south of England the rural population, led mostly by men of the yeoman class, staged a series of demonstrations against changing patterns of tenancy and land use. They were protesting partly against violations of the law, but far more against legal practices which they considered to be contrary to natural justice, and to their own economic interests. Two generations ago, historians tended to take these complaints at their face value, and concluded that there had indeed been widespread abuse of the poor and vulnerable by rich landlords and sheep ranchers.[10] However, more recent and detailed research has not supported this view. Individual examples of flagrant abuse can be cited, but the more general breakdown of trust and cooperation between lords and tenants was not caused by a sudden epidemic of irresponsible economic egotism on the part of the former. It was predominantly the result of a steady increase in the population, which had been going on since the late fifteenth century, and which had pushed up the demand for tenancies above the level of supply. Consequently changes of land use which had taken place half a century before, and which had caused no comment at the time, became grievances. More recently pressure on the consumer market accompanied by debasement of the coinage, which began in 1545 to pay for Henry VIII's wars, had caused dramatic and unprecedented inflation. As a result, customary rents fell far below current economic values, and when leases fell in landlords inevitably raised rents as the price of renewal. This aroused an irrational fury among traditionalists who could not, or would not, understand the economics of leasing, and some landlords refused renewal altogether rather than face such a storm of complaint.

The agrarian crisis which reached its peak in Norfolk in 1549 arose therefore from a clash of cultures rather from the 'conspiracy of rich men' which Sir Thomas More had invoked. On the one hand stood the traditional Christian doctrine of the stewardship of wealth, which proclaimed that it was the responsibility of the rich or powerful man to protect and succour the weak. This was a view shared by government, by humanist scholars, and by fashionable Protestant preachers such as Hugh Latimer. Unfortunately it was a static philosophy, based upon the same foundations as the just price. Both theories assumed a stable economic situation in which customs, including payments, could remain unchanged for generations. Such stability made change appear immoral, and branded anyone, whether landlord or craftsman, who increased his prices as an enemy of the commonwealth. On the other side stood economic reality. It was not the fault of landlords, merchants, or even of bankers, that the value of money had dropped by 50 per cent in a decade. Each had to cope with that reality, and stay afloat to the best of his ability, in doing which each became the scapegoat for other men's hardships. This had nothing to do with 'capitalism' in the nineteenth- or twentieth-century sense. The investment of money was hardly ever in question. What was in question was the extent to which economic self-interest should be allowed to determine behaviour. As Francois Van der Delft, the Imperial ambassador, pointed out with unwonted shrewdness in July 1549, the peasants were demanding things both reasonable and unreasonable, and among the unreasonable demands he listed a return of rents and prices to where they had stood in the reign of King Henry VII.[11] It is not surprising that labourers and tenant farmers should have failed to appreciate the subtleties of a market economy, but the moral assault upon the aristocracy carried out by educated reformers such as John Hales and Robert Crowley had a very serious effect upon an already fragile social situation. Impersonal economic forces, which produced a genuine, if not altogether justified, sense of grievance, combined with the uncertainties of the Protector's policy and this heady rhetoric to produce a crisis which left a long shadow over the following decade.

There were local differences. Social animus seems to have been sharper in Devon than it was in East Anglia. The gentry were more resolute and better organised in Wiltshire than they were in Oxfordshire. In the Midlands enclosure of arable land was the main issue, in Norfolk the enclosure of commons. A powerful social conservatism, however, seems to have been general, and the local differences owed little to any sense of regional identity. Manorial custom might vary from one area to another, but anxieties did not focus upon one sort of custom. The fear was that customs in general were being undermined, and that fear was justified. However it was not the cynical manipulations of antisocial men which was bringing this about, so much as inflation and demography. Paradoxically the Tudor governments, which repeatedly and sincerely endeavoured to support traditional legal and economic structures, were also partly responsible for their decay. Inviolable manorial custom was an aspect of that social structure which also embraced Good Lordship, and the power of the great regional affinities. Having undermined that structure in pursuit of national unity and royal power, it proved impossible to sustain upon a selective basis. It was no coincidence that great affinities had recently been destroyed in both the areas which got most seriously out of control in 1549. Moreover no sixteenth-century government could run a planned economy, however grandiose its pretensions in other respects, and in the event the Tudors were constrained to leave the economy in the hands of those same citizens and gentlemen who ran the commissions of the peace, and represented the realm in the House of Commons.

With the dangerous exception of Ireland, Tudor government worked. In England it worked because successive monarchs were able to dismantle the great bastard feudal affinities, and reinvent the nobility in a service mode. At the same time they were able to create a partnership with the gentry and the elites of the major towns, which established a ruling class of remarkable comprehensiveness and durability – a gentry commonwealth. This was not achieved without setbacks, and it was not proof against the political follies of the Stuarts, but as long as the dynasty lasted England enjoyed a stability unequalled in Europe. In Wales and the smaller dependent territories it worked because the Crown took the local elites into partnership, and in the case of Wales adopted aspects of its distinctive culture as part of the realm's identity. English regional cultures were weak, and political provincialism in the French or German mode was almost non-existent, while Wales lacked a powerful indigenous nobility to provide alternative leadership at the highest level. Ireland, on the other hand, had both a distinctive culture and a powerful nobility. These two things were not at first associated, because the Anglo-Irish magnates of the early Tudor period were not leaders of the native Irish. However, dissatisfaction with the questionable loyalty of such men as Ormond and Kildare, culminating in the rebellion of Silken Thomas, tempted the English Council into a fatal ambition. The attempt to assert more direct rule from England drove a wedge between the Crown and the Anglo-Irish, which was exacerbated by the fact that there were no commissions of the peace to form vehicles of partnership. This could have been overcome if St Leger's conciliatory attempts to involve the native Irish chieftains in the government of the whole kingdom had been successful. However, impatience in Westminster combined with a lack of sympathy in the Pale to frustrate this hopeful initiative. Once the English Council had decided, at the beginning of Elizabeth's reign, that only a policy of gradual conquest and partial settlement would reduce Ireland to order, then all the elements of Irish identity became anti-English, and the 'old English' began to adopt them. Irish dress, law, language, and eventually the Catholic religion, all became symbols of resistance to English rule, in a manner which they had never been in the earlier period. The Irish were neither rich nor militarily strong, so when the English put their minds and resources to it, they could always regain control, as they did at the end of the Tyrone rebellion. Spain and the papacy were interested in Ireland mainly as a lever against England, and never had any serious intention of supporting Tyrone's ambition for an independent state. Consequently when Elizabeth died, Ireland was subdued but unreconciled. The developing sense of national identity, already so noticeable in the rest of the realm, was not shared in Ireland. There was no partnership but an increasingly alien rule, which every so often boiled over into hatred. The failure was one of policy, not of circumstance, but it also serves to emphasise how much credit the Tudors should be given for their achievement in their other and greater kingdom.

Notes

1. Grafton, *Chronicle* (ed. 1809) p. 206.
2. F. Rose-Troup, *The Western Rebellion of 1549* (1913) p. 493.
3. G. Dyfnallt Owen, *Elizabethan Wales* (1964) pp. 198–231.
4. R. A. Griffiths and R. S. Thomas, *The Making of the Tudor Dynasty* (1987) pp. 179–95.
5. Glanmor Williams, *Welsh Reformation Essays* (Cardiff, 1967) pp. 191–205.
6. John Hacket, *Scrinia reservata: a memorial offered to the great deservings of John Williams, D.D.* (1693).
7. Williams, *Welsh Reformation Essays*, pp. 55-6.
8. M. E. James, *Family, Lineage and Civil Society* (1974) pp. 52–67; James, 'The concept of order and the northern rising, 1569', *Past and Present*, 48 (1970) pp. 49-83; James, 'English politics and the concept of honour', *Past and Present*, supplement 3 (1978).
9. C. Haigh, *Reformation and Resistance in Tudor Lancashire* (1975).
10. R. H. Tawney, *Religion and the Rise of Capitalism* (1938).
11. G. A. Bergenroth (ed.), *Calendar of State Papers, Spanish*, vol. IX, pp. 405–9.

1   Dioceses before the Reformation

The heavy line shows the boundaries of the new sees founded
by Henry VIII in 1541 and recognised by Pope Paul IV in 1555.

The grey marks the area of the see of Westminister, i.e. Middlesex,
founded by Henry VIII in 1541 and suppressed by Edward VI in 1550.

☨ Cathedral city

2   New Dioceses Created by Henry VIII

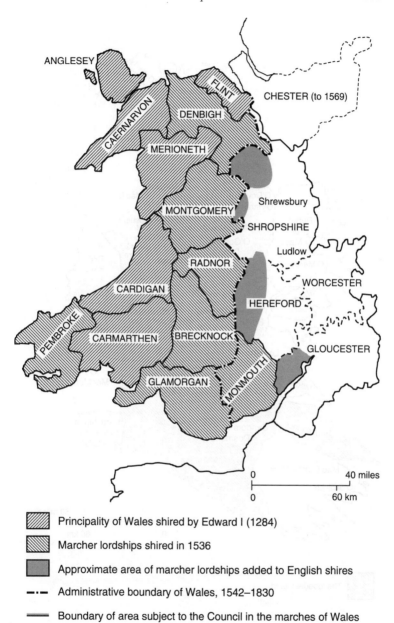

Legend:

- Principality of Wales shired by Edward I (1284)
- Marcher lordships shired in 1536
- Approximate area of marcher lordships added to English shires
- —·— Administrative boundary of Wales, 1542–1830
- ——— Boundary of area subject to the Council in the marches of Wales

3   Wales: The Union with England, 1536–43

4   Ireland *c.* 1530

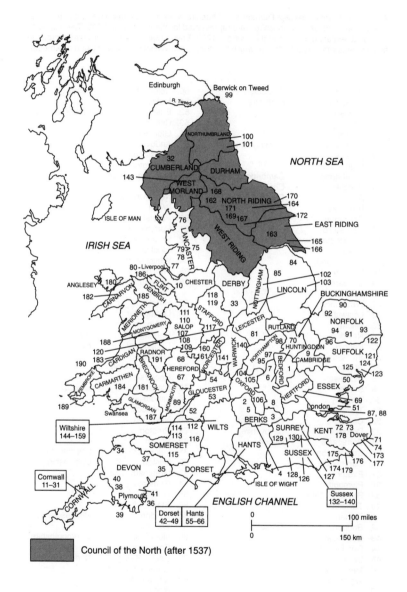

Edinburgh   Berwick on Tweed
                99
   R. Tweed

NORTHUMBRLAND   100
                101

      32   NORTH SEA
   CUMBERLAND   DURHAM
143
        WEST   168
      MORLAND
        162   NORTH RIDING   170
             171   164
         169167   172
ISLE OF MAN   76   EAST RIDING
                     163
IRISH SEA   WEST RIDING   165
                                    166
        79 75
        78   84
80 - Liverpool 77   85   102
ANGLESEY 180 186 CHESTER DERBY   103
            FLINT   NOTTINGHAM   LINCOLN   BUCKINGHAMSHIRE
182   CARNARVON 10   90
       DENBIGH   118
                 119   33
        MERIONETH 111   92
                  110   STAFFORD LEICESTER NORFOLK
        MONTGOMERY SALOP 117   94 91 93
188   107   RUTLAND   122
120   RADNOR 108 81   NORTHAMPTON 70 SUFFOLK 121
   CARDIGAN 109 160   98 HUNTINGDON 124
183 191 68161 141 WARWICK 97 9 125 123
190 PEMBROKE HEREFORD   95 CAMBRIDGE 50
   CARMARTHEN 67 54 OXFORD 104 1
184 181   GLOUCESTER 105 7 6 HERTFORD ESSEX
        GLAMORGAN 89 53 2 106 8   69
189   Swansea 187 52   5   London 51
                                         87, 88
Wiltshire 114 112   3   SURREY 72 73
144-159   113 WILTS   BERKS 129 130 KENT 178 Dover
        116   HANTS   175   71
   34   SOMERSET   74
        37 115   SUSSEX 174 173
Cornwall DEVON 35 DORSET   127 179 177
11-31   40   4 128   176
        38   ISLE OF WIGHT 126
   Plymouth 41   Sussex
CORNWALL 36   ENGLISH CHANNEL   132-140
        39
      Dorset Hants   0   100 miles
      42-49 55-66
                    0   150 km

Council of the North (after 1537)

5   Tudor England and Wales: Counties and Parliamentary Boroughs

Map 5: Counties and parliamentary representation

All English counties, except Durham and Cheshire, were represented throughout the period. The Welsh counties and Cheshire were represented for the first time in 1539. The map shows the parliamentary boroughs as they were in 1600. Each English constituency was represented by two members, except London, which had four. Each Welsh constituency had one member.

1.	Bedford	Bedfordshire	
2.	Abingdon	Berkshire	
3.	Windsor	"	
4.	Reading	"	
5.	Wallingford	"	
6.	Aylesbury	Buckinghamshire	
7.	Buckingham	"	
8.	High Wycombe	"	
9.	Cambridge	Cambridgeshire	
10.	Chester	Cheshire	
11.	Bodmin	Cornwall	
12.	Bossiney	"	
13.	Callington	"	
14.	Camelford	"	
15.	Launceston	"	
16.	Fowey	"	
17.	Grampound	"	
18.	Helston	"	
19.	Liskeard	"	
20.	East Looe	"	
21.	West Looe	"	
22.	Lostwithiel	"	
23.	Mitchell	"	
24.	Newport	"	
25.	Penryn	"	
26.	St. Germans	"	
27.	St.Ives	"	
28.	St.Mawes	"	
29.	Saltash	"	
30.	Tregony	"	
31.	Truro	"	
32.	Carlisle	Cumberland	
33.	Derby	Derbyshire	
34.	Barnstaple	Devon	
35.	Bere Alston	"	
36.	Dartmouth	"	
37.	Exeter	"	
38.	Plymouth	"	
39.	Plymouth Erle	"	
40.	Tavistock	"	
41.	Totnes	"	
42.	Bridport	Dorset	
43.	Corfe Castle	"	
44.	Dorchester	"	
45.	Lyme Regis	"	
46.	Melcombe Regis/ Weymouth	"	
47.	Poole	"	
48.	Shaftesbury	"	
49.	Wareham	"	
50.	Colchester	Essex	
51.	Maldon	"	
52.	Bristol	Gloucestershire	
53.	Cirencester	"	
54.	Gloucester	"	
55.	Andover	Hampshire	
56.	Christchurch	"	
57.	Lymington	"	
58.	Newport, Isle of Wight	"	
59.	Newtown, Isle of Wight	"	
60.	Petersfield	"	
61.	Portsmouth	"	
62.	Southampton	"	
63.	Stockbridge	"	
64.	Whitchurch	"	
65.	Winchester	"	
66.	Yarmouth, Isle of Wight	"	
67.	Hereford	Herefordshire	
68.	Leominster	"	
69.	St.Albans	Hertfordshire	
70.	Huntingdon	Huntingdonshire	
71.	Canterbury	Kent	
72.	Maidstone	"	
73.	Queenborough	"	
74.	Rochester	"	
75.	Clitheroe	Lancashire	
76.	Lancaster	"	
77.	Liverpool	"	
78.	Newtown	"	
79.	Preston	"	
80.	Wigan	"	
81.	Leicester	Leicestershire	
82.	Boston	Lincolnshire	
83.	Grantham	"	
84.	Grimsby	"	
85.	Lincoln	"	
86.	Stamford	"	
87.	London	Middlesex	
88.	Westminster	"	
89.	Monmouth Boroughs	Monmouthshire	
90.	Castle Rising	Norfolk	
91.	Great Yarmouth	"	
92.	Kings Lynn	"	
93.	Norwich	"	
94.	Thetford	"	
95.	Brackley	Northamptonshire	

96.	Higham Ferrers	Northamptonshire	146.	Cricklade	Wiltshire
97.	Northampton	"	147.	Devizes	"
98.	Peterborough	"	148.	Downton	"
99.	Berwick-on-Tweed	Northumberland	149.	Great Bedwyn	"
			150.	Heytesbury	"
100.	Morpeth	"	151.	Hindon	"
101.	Newcastle-upon-Tyne	"	152.	Ludgershall	"
			153.	Malmesbury	"
102.	East Retford	Nottinghamshire	154.	Marlborough	"
103.	Nottingham	"	155.	Old Sarum	"
104.	Banbury	Oxfordshire	156.	Salisbury	"
105.	Woodstock	"	157.	Westbury	"
106.	Oxford	"	158.	Wilton	"
107.	Bishop's Castle	Shropshire	159.	Wootton Bassett	"
108.	Bridgenorth	"	160.	Droitwich	Worcestershire
109.	Ludlow	"	161.	Worcester	"
110.	Much Wenlock	"	162.	Aldborough	Yorkshire
111.	Shrewsbury	"	163.	Beverley	"
112.	Bath	Somerset	164.	Boroughbridge	"
113.	Bridgewater	"	165.	Hedon	"
114.	Minehead	"	166.	Kingston-on-Hull	"
115.	Taunton	"	167.	Knaresborough	"
116.	Wells	"	168.	Richmond	"
117.	Lichfield	Staffordshire	169.	Ripon	"
118.	Newcastle-under-Lyme	"	170.	Scarborough	"
			171.	Thirsk	"
119.	Stafford	"	172.	York	"
120.	Tamworth	"	173.	Dover	Cinq Ports
121.	Aldeburgh	Suffolk	174.	Hastings	"
122.	Dunwich	"	175.	Hythe	"
123.	Ipswich	"	176.	New Romney	"
124.	Orford	"	177.	Rye	"
125.	Sudbury	"	178.	Sandwich	"
126.	Bletchingley	Surrey	179.	Winchelsea	"
127.	Gatton	"	180.	Beaumaris	Anglesey
128.	Guildford	"	181.	Brecon Boroughs	Brecknockshire
129.	Hazelmere	"	182.	Caernarfon Boroughs	Caernarfonshire
130.	Reigate	"			
131.	Southwark	"	183.	Cardigan Boroughs	Cardiganshire
132.	Arundel	Sussex			
133.	Bramber	"	184.	Carmarthen Boroughs	Carmarthenshire
134.	Chichester	"			
135.	East Grinstead	"	185.	Denbigh Boroughs	Denbighshire
136.	Horsham	"			
137.	Lewes	"	186.	Flint Boroughs	Flintshire
138.	Midhurst	"	187.	Cardiff Boroughs	Glamorgan
139.	New Shoreham	"	188.	Montgomery Boroughs	Montgomeryshire
140.	Steyning	"			
141.	Coventry	Warwickshire	189.	Haverford West	Pembrokeshire
142.	Warwick	"	190.	Pembroke Boroughs	"
143.	Appleby	Westmorland			
144.	Calne	Wiltshire	191.	New Radnor Boroughs	Radnorshire
145.	Chippenham	"			

Select Bibliography

The range of reading possibilities is enormous, but the period has been well served by bibliographers, and almost comprehensive coverage can be obtained by consulting Conyers Read, *Bibliography of British History: Tudor Period, 1485–1603*, 2nd edn (1959, reprinted 1978) for all works published before 1958; the Institute of Historical Research series *Writings on British History* for works published between 1958 and 1974; and the Royal Historical Society's *Annual Bibliography of British History* since 1975. There are also useful and wide-ranging bibliographies attached to several recent textbooks, notably J. A. Guy, *Tudor England* (1988).

The following suggestions are listed under the topic headings of the chapters. Several works are relevant to more than one topic, but for reasons of clarity and space are listed only once. Works of particular importance have been briefly annotated. Source material and published documents have not been included here, except in footnote references, but a small number of texts are fundamental to an understanding of contemporary political theory and practice: notably Sir John Fortescue's *De Laudibus Legum Anglie* (ed. S. B. Chrimes, 1949); the same author's *The Governance of England* (ed. C. Plummer, Oxford, 1885); Stephen Gardiner's *De Vera Obedientia Oratio* (ed. Pierre Jannelle in *Obedience in Church and State*, 1930); Sir Thomas Smith's *De Republica Anglorum* (ed. Mary Dewar, Cambridge, 1982); Edmund Dudley's *Tree of Commonwealth* (ed. D. M. Brodie, 1948); *The Commonweal of the Realm of England* (ed. E. Lamond, 1949); and William Lambarde, *Eirenarcha, or the Office of the Justice of the Peace* (1602). Because these works are of general importance, they have not been listed under topics.

GENERAL WORKS

C. S. L. Davies, *Peace, Print and Protestantism, 1450–1558* (1978) – Strong on the continuities between medieval and early modern England.

G. R. Elton, *England under the Tudors*, 3rd edn (1993) – Latest update of the 1955 classic; still useful.

G. R. Elton, *The Tudor Constitution*, 2nd edn (Cambridge, 1982) – Indispensable for central government, but thin on local government. Ignores the court.

G. R. Elton, *Reform and Reformation, 1485–1558* (1977) – Mostly about Henry VIII. A partial rethink of *The Tudor Revolution in Government*.

S. J. Gunn, *Early Tudor Government, 1485–1558* (1995) – The latest interpretation. Footnotes contain a wealth of references to recent secondary works.

J. A. Guy, *Tudor England* (Oxford, 1988) – The most recent complete textbook. Excellent digest of research before 1987.

Dale Hoak (ed.), *Tudor Political Culture* (Cambridge, 1995) – A very good collection of essays, mostly on imagery and ceremonies.

W. S. Holdsworth, *The History of English Law* (Vol. I, ed. S. B. Chrimes, 1956; vols. IV and V, 3rd edn, 1945) – Still the best reference book for the tangles of the common law.

D. M. Loades, *Politics and the Nation, 1450–1660* 4th edn (1992) – A longer view, presenting a theory of the rise and fall of the Tudor state.

Felix Makower, *The Constitutional History of the Church of England* (1895) – Useful reference book on ecclesiastical structures.

A. G. R. Smith, *The Formation of a Nation State, 1529–1660* (1984) – Succinct interpretation, with a wealth of information in appendices.

J. A. F. Thompson, *The Transformation of Medieval England, 1370–1529* (1983) – Another useful view of the continuities.

Penry Williams, *The Tudor Regime* (Oxford, 1979) – The best and most comprehensive analysis of Tudor society in its relationship with government at all levels.

Penry Williams, *The Later Tudors: England 1547–1603* (Oxford, 1995) – A substantial and valuable analysis. A thematic interpretation on a political framework.

Joyce Youings, *Sixteenth-Century England* (1984) – A social and economic survey. Rich in anecdotes and case studies.

PREAMBLE: A PERSONAL MONARCHY

S. Anglo, *Images of Tudor Kingship* (1992).

S. B. Chrimes, *Henry VII* (1973) – Still the best study of the reign, although there are now many competitors.

R. A. Griffiths, *The Reign of Henry VI* (1981).

R. A. Griffiths and R. S. Thomas, *The Making of the Tudor Dynasty* (Gloucester, 1985).

J. R. Lander, *Crown and Nobility, 1450–1509* (1976) – The most comprehensive of Lander's many useful works in this field.

D. M. Loades, *The Reign of Mary Tudor*, 2nd edn (1991) – The only full study of the reign.

C. Lloyd and S. Thurley, *Henry VIII: Images of a Tudor King* (1990).

W. MacCaffrey, *Elizabeth I* (1993) – The summary of a lifetime's work on the subject. Full of insights.

C. Ross, *Edward IV* (1974).

C. Ross, *Richard III* (1981) – A judicious and learned treatment of a controversial figure.

J. J. Scarisbrick, *Henry VIII* (1968) – Still the best general study of the man and his reign.

R. Strong, *The Cult of Elizabeth* (1977) – The most accessible of Strong's many works in this field.

1 THE NATURE OF AUTHORITY

M. Axton, *The Queen's Two Bodies* (1977).

J. M. W. Bean, *From Lord to Patron: Lordship in Late Medieval England* (Manchester, 1989).

J. G. Bellamy, *Bastard Feudalism and the Law* (Portland, Oregon, 1989).

G. W. Bernard, *Power and the Early Tudor Nobility* (Brighton, 1985) – A case study of the 4th and 5th Earls of Shrewsbury, but with wider implications.

J. H. Burns, *Lordship, Kingship and Empire: The Idea of Monarchy, 1400–1525* (Oxford, 1992) – A penetrating study, central to an understanding of renaissance monarchy.

F. Caspari, *Humanism and the Social Order in Tudor England* (New York, 1954).

S. B. Chrimes, *English Constitutional Ideas in the Fifteenth Century* (1936).

M. M. Condon, 'Ruling elites in the reign of Henry VII' in C. Ross (ed.), *Patronage, Pedigree and Power in Late Medieval England* (1979) – A valuable insight into a somewhat understudied subject.

P. Corrigan and D. Sayer, *The Great Arch: English State Formation as Cultural Revolution* (1985) – A historical and sociological examination of the idea of the state in England over a long period.

E. Duffy, *The Stripping of the Altars* (Princeton, 1992) – The best description and analysis of late medieval English religion.

G. R. Elton, *The Tudor Revolution in Government* (Cambridge, 1953) – Elton's original challenging thesis on the career of Thomas Cromwell. Now itself challenged in many respects, but essential reading.

G. R. Elton, *Reform and Renewal* (1973) – Thomas Cromwell as intellectual and visionary. Persuasive if not totally convincing.

A. Everitt, 'Social mobility in Early Modern England', *Past and Present*, 33 (1966).

A. B. Ferguson. *The Indian Summer of English Chivalry: Studies in the Decline and Transformation of Chivalric Idealism* (1949).

J. A. Guy, 'Thomas Cromwell and the intellectual origins of the Henrician Revolution', in A. Fox and J. A. Guy (eds), *Reassessing the Henrician Age: Humanism, Politics and Reform, 1500–1550* (1990) – A discreet critique of Elton.

C. Haigh, *English Reformations* (Oxford, 1993) – Argues that Protestantism was slowly and unevenly accepted as a result of political pressure.

G. L. Harriss, 'Medieval Government and Statecraft', *Past and Present*, 24 (1963) – Argues that nothing very new happened under the Tudors.

R. A. Houlbrooke, *The English Family, 1450–1700* (1984) – Examines structures and attitudes as well as economics and kinship.

S. L. Jansen, *Political Protest and Prophecy under Henry VIII* (1991).

R. Koebner, 'The Imperial Crown of this realm: Henry VIII, Constantine the Great and Polydore Vergil', *Bulletin of the Institute of Historical Research*, 26 (1953).

J. R. Lander, *The Limitations of English Monarchy in the Later Middle Ages* (1989).

T. F. Mayer, *Thomas Starkey and the Commonweal: Humanist Politics and Religion in the Reign of Henry VIII* (1989) – An examination of the 'Commonwealth' critique of mid-Tudor government.

K. B. MacFarlane, *The Nobility of Later Medieval England* (Oxford, 1973) – A seminal and extremely influential interpretation.

Helen Miller, *Henry VIII and the English Nobility* (Oxford, 1986).

S. Lockwood, 'Marsilius of Padua and the case for the royal ecclesiastical supremacy', *Transactions of the Royal Historical Society*, 6th series, 1 (1991) – Demonstrates how Marsilius's ideas were adapted to fit English circumstances.

Richard Rex, *Henry VIII and the English Reformation* (1993).

Quentin Skinner, *The Foundations of Modern Political Thought* (Cambridge, 1978) – In two volumes; as comprehensive as its title suggests. Not very original on English thinking.

A. J. Slavin, 'The Tudor state, reformation and understanding change', in P. A. Fideler and T. F. Mayer (eds), *Political Thought and the Tudor Commonwealth: Deep Structure, Discourse and Disguise*, (1992).

L. Stone, *The Family, Sex and Marriage in England, 1500–1800* (1977).

E. Surtz and V. Murphy, *The Divorce Tracts of Henry VIII* (1988).

K. Thomas, *Religion and the Decline of Magic* (1971) – Fundamental study of cultural transformation.

W. Ullman, 'This realm of England is an Empire', *Journal of Ecclesiastical History*, 30 (1979).

A. Wall, 'Patterns of politics in England, 1558–1628', *Historical Journal*, 31 (1988).

2 STRUCTURES

J. M. W. Bean, *The Decline of English Feudalism, 1215–1540* (Manchester, 1968) – Has been effectively criticised, but still useful.

J. G. Bellamy, *Crime and Public Order in England in the Later Middle Ages* (1973).

G. W. Bernard (ed.), *The Tudor Nobility* (Manchester, 1992) – A valuable collection of essays, covering a number of peerage families.

M. Blatcher, *The Court of King's Bench, 1450–1550* (1978) – The best treatment of the subject.

L. O. Boynton, *The Elizabethan Militia* (1967).

S. E. Brigden, *London and the Reformation* (Oxford, 1989) – An exhaustive, and very informative, treatment of the subject.

C. Carpenter, *Locality and Polity: A Study of Warwickshire Landed Society, 1401–1499* (Cambridge, 1992) – A valuable and highly praised case study of a county society.

P. Clark and P. Slack (eds), *English Towns in Transition, 1500–1700* (1976).

C. H. Clough (ed.), *Profession, Vocation and Culture in Later Medieval England* (1982).

P. Collinson, 'The monarchical republic of Queen Elizabeth I', *Bulletin of the John Rylands Library*, 69 (1986–7).

B. Coward, *The Stanleys, Lords Stanley and Earls of Derby, 1385–1672* (Manchester, 1983).

J. A. Guy, *The Cardinal's Court: The Impact of Thomas Wolsey in Star Chamber* (Brighton, 1977) – The best examination of the working of Tudor conciliar jurisdiction.

A. Hassell Smith, *County and Court: Government and Politics in Norfolk, 1558–1603* (Oxford, 1974).

R. H. Helmholz, *Canon Law and the Church of England* (Cambridge, 1987).

R. A. Houlbrooke, *Church Courts and the People during the English Reformation, 1520–1570* (1979).

R. W. Hoyle (ed.), *The Military Survey of Gloucestershire, 1522* (1993) – Intended for both military and taxation purposes, this is one of the few returns to have survived.

E. W. Ives, *The Common Lawyers of Pre-reformation England* (Cambridge, 1983) – A case study of Thomas Kebell rather than a comprehensive survey, but highly informative.

M. E. James, *Family, Lineage and Civil Society: A Study of Society Politics and Mentality in the Durham Region, 1500–1640* (Oxford, 1974).

M. E. James, *Society, Politics and Culture: Studies in Early Modern England* (1986).

W. J. Jones, *The Elizabethan Court of Chancery* (1967).

E. Kerridge, *The Agrarian Problem in the Sixteenth Century and After* (1969) – A brief but lucid explanation of the nature of tenures and the economic realities of the rural society.

I. S. Leadam, *Select Cases before the Court of Star Chamber, 1477–1509* (Selden Society, 16, 1903).

D. N. J. MacCulloch, *Suffolk and the Tudors: Politics and Religion in an English County, 1500–1600* (Oxford, 1986) – Widely acclaimed as the best study of a sixteenth-century county community.

D. Marcombe, *A Small Town: Retford, 1500–1640* (1991).

K. Mertes, *The English Noble Household, 1250–1600* (1988).

D. A. L. Morgan, 'The King's Affinity in the policy of Yorkist England', *Transactions of the Royal Historical Society*, 5th series, 23 (1973).

S. Rappaport, *Worlds within Worlds: Structures of Life in Sixteenth-Century London* (Cambridge, 1989) – A detailed analysis of the government of England's only true city.

C. Rawcliffe, 'The great lords as peace keepers: arbitration by English noblemen and their councils in the late middle ages', in J. A. Guy and H. G. Beale (eds), *Law and Social Change in British History* (1984).

W. C. Richardson, *A History of the Court of Augmentations* (Morganstown, West VA. 1961) – A valuable study, but some of its conclusions now need revision.

W. C. Richardson, *Tudor Chamber Administration* (Morganstown, West VA. 1952).

A. L. Rowse, *Tudor Cornwall*, 2nd edn (1969) – Still one of the best studies of an English county.

R. S. Schofield, 'Taxation and the political limits of the Tudor State', in C. Cross , D. Loades and J. Scarisrick (eds), *Law and Government under the Tudors* (Cambridge, 1987).

R. B. Smith, *Land and Politics in the England of Henry VIII: The West Riding of Yorkshire 1530–1546* (Oxford, 1970).

L. Stone, *The Crisis of the Aristocracy, 1558–1640* (Oxford, 1965) – A major work of reference rather than a monograph. Some of Stone's conclusions have been challenged, but his case studies remain invaluable.

J. A. F. Thompson, *The Early Tudor Church and Society, 1485–1529* (1993).

R. Tittler, 'The incorporation of boroughs, 1540–1558', *History*, 62 (1977).

G. S. Thomson, *Lords Lieutenant in the Sixteenth Century* (1923) – Still the only specific study of the subject.

B. P. Woolfe, *The Crown Lands, 1461–1536* (1970).

3   THE COUNCIL

C. G. Bayne and W. H. Dunham (eds), *Select Cases in the Council of Henry VII* (Selden Society, 75, 1964).

J. F. Baldwin, *The King's Council in the Middle Ages* (1913).

B. L. Beer, *Northumberland* (Kent, Ohio, 1973) – Good on the Dudley estates, rather thin on his career, particularly before 1550.

A. L. Brown, 'The King's councillors in fifteenth century England', *Transactions of the Royal Historical Society*, 5th series, 19 (1969).

M. L. Bush, *The Government Policy of Protector Somerset* (1975) – A persuasive argument for the priority of Somersert's Scottish policy.

G .R. Elton, 'Tudor Government: Points of Contact: The Council', in *Studies in Tudor and Stuart Politics and Government*, Vol. III (1983).

J. A. Guy, 'The Privy Council: revolution or evolution', in D. Starkey and C. Coleman (eds) *Revolution Reassessed* (1986) – The most effective critique of Elton's thesis.

J. A. Guy, 'The King's Council and political participation', in A. Fox and J. A. Guy, *Reassessing the Henrician Age* (Oxford, 1986).

P. J. Gwyn, *The King's Cardinal: The Rise and Fall of Thomas Wolsey* (1990) – The fullest and most recent account of his career, but a rather ponderous and undiscriminating approach.

E. H. Harbison, *Rival Ambassadors at the Court of Queen Mary* (Princeton, 1940) – Based largely on research in Paris and Besancon, a model piece of research, which has stood the test of time.

D. E. Hoak, *The King's Council in the reign of Edward VI* (Cambridge, 1976) – The standard work on the subject.

D. E. Hoak, 'Two revolutions in Tudor government: the formation and organisation of Mary I's Privy Council', in D. Starkey and C. Coleman (eds), *Revolution Reassessed* (1986).

P. J. Holmes, 'The Great Council in the reign of Henry VII', *English Historical Review*, 101 (1986).

P. J. Holmes, 'The last Tudor Great Councils', *Historical Journal*, 33 (1990).

J. R. Lander, 'Council, administration and councillors, 1461–1485', *Bulletin of the Institute of Historical Research*, 32 (1959).

J. Loach, *Protector Somerset: a reassessment* (Bangor, 1994).

D. M. Loades, *John Dudley, Duke of Northumberland* (1996) – A brief sketch.

W. MacCaffrey, *The Shaping of the Elizabethan Regime . . . 1558–1572* (1969) – The best account of the construction of Elizabeth's court and Council.

M. B. Pulman, *The Elizabethan Privy Council in the 1570s* (Berkeley, Calif., 1971) – The only detailed study of the council at work in any decade of the reign.

Conyers Read, *Mr. Secretary Cecil and Queen Elizabeth* (1955).

Glyn Redworth, *In Defence of the Church Catholic: The Life of Stephen Gardiner* (Oxford, 1990) – The best and most recent study of this central and problematic character.

R. Somerville, 'Henry VII's Council Learned in the Law', *English Historical Review*, 54 (1939).

D. Starkey, 'Court, council and nobility in Tudor England', in R. G. Asch and A. M. Birke (eds), *Princes, Patronage and the Nobility: the Court at the beginning of the Modern Age, 1450–1650* (1991).

R. Virgoe, 'The composition of the king's council, 1437–1461', *Bulletin of the Institute of Historical Research*, 43 (1970).

4   THE ROYAL COMMISSIONS

J. D. Alsop, 'The Revenue Commission of 1552', *Historical Journal*, 22 (1979).

C. Arnold, 'The commission of the peace for the West Riding of Yorkshire, 1437–1509', in A. J. Pollard (ed.) *Property and Politics: Essays in Later Medieval English History*, (1984).

J. S. Cockburn, *A History of the English Assizes from 1558 to 1714* (Oxford, 1972).

J. C. K. Cornwall, *Wealth and Society in Early Sixteenth-Century England* (1988).

J. H. Gleason, *The Justice of the Peace in England, 1558–1640* (Oxford, 1969).

J. J. Goring, 'Social change and military decline in Mid-Tudor England', *History*, 60 (1975).

J. H. Hexter, 'Storm over the gentry', in *Reappraisals in History* (1961) – Skilful deflation of the notorious controversy between R. H. Tawney and Hugh Trevor Roper.

M. J. Ingram, 'Communities and courts: law and disorder in early seventeenth century Wiltshire', in J. S. Cockburn (ed.), *Crime in England, 1500–1800* (1977).

J. R. Lander, *English Justices of the Peace, 1461–1509* (1989).

G. Dyfnallt Owen, *Elizabethan Wales* (Cardiff, 1964).

B. H. Putnam (ed.), *Early Treatises on the Practice of Justices of the Peace in the fifteenth and sixteenth centuries* (1924).

W. C. Richardson, *The Report of the Royal Commission of 1552* (1974) – An important investigation into the royal finances, edited with a commentary which has been criticised and revised by J. D. Alsop.

J. Samaha, *Law and Order in Historical Perspective: The Case of Elizabethan Essex* (1974).

H. Thomas, *A History of Wales, 1485–1603* (Cardiff, 1972).

F. A. Youngs, 'Towards petty sessions: Tudor J.P.s and the division of counties', in. D. J. Guth and J. W. McKenna (eds), *Tudor Rule and Revolution* (1982).

M. Zell, 'Early Tudor J.P.s at work', *Archaeologia Cantiana*, 93 (1977).

5 THE PARLIAMENT

I. W. Archer, 'The London lobbies in the late sixteenth century', *Historical Journal*, 31 (1988).

D. M. Dean and N. L. Jones (eds), *The Parliaments of Elizabethan England* (1990).

G. R. Elton, '"The Body of the Whole Realm": Parliament and Representation in Medieval and Tudor England', in *Studies in Tudor and Stuart Politics and Government*, Vol. II (1974).

G. R. Elton, 'Tudor Government: points of contact: the Parliament', in *Studies in Tudor and Stuart Politics and Government*, Vol. III (1983).

G. R. Elton, *The Parliament of England, 1559–1581* (Cambridge, 1986) – The most recent and complete analysis of these parliaments. Strong insistence upon business before politics.

M. A. R. Graves, *Early Tudor Parliaments* (1990) – A brief but informative introduction.

M. A. R. Graves, *The Tudor Parliaments: Crown Lords and Commons 1485–1603* (1985).

M. A. R. Graves, *The House of Lords in the Parliaments of Edward VI and Mary* (Cambridge, 1981) – An important research monograph.

M. A. R. Graves, *Elizabethan Parliaments, 1559–1601* (1987).

M. A. R. Graves, *Thomas Norton: the Parliament Man* (Oxford, 1995) – A valuable discussion of the manner in which the Elizabethan council sought to manage the House of Commons.

A. D. K. Hawkwood, 'The enfranchisement of constituencies, 1509–1558', *Parliamentary History*, 10 (1991).

N. L. Jones, *Faith by Statute* (1982) – Now the 'orthodox', interpretation of the Elizabethan settlement; argues that Elizabeth got substantially what she wanted. Attacked by recent revisionists.

S. Lambert, 'Precedure in the House of Commons in the early Stuart period', *English Historical Review*, 95 (1980).

S. E. Lehmberg, *The Reformation Parliament, 1529–1536* (Cambridge, 1970).

S. E. Lehmberg, *The Later Parliaments of Henry VIII, 1536–1545* (Cambridge, 1977).

J. Loach, *Parliament and the Crown in the Reign of Mary Tudor* (1986). The best and most detailed analysis of these meetings.

J. Loach, *Parliament under the Tudors* (Oxford, 1991) – Another introduction, but taking a different line from Graves.

J. W. McKenna, 'The myth of parliamentary sovereignty in late medieval England', *English Historical Review*, 94 (1979).

H. Miller, 'London and parliament in the reign of Henry VIII', *Bulletin of the Institute of Historical Research*, 35 (1962).

H. Miller, 'Lords and Commons: relations between the two Houses of Parliament, 1509–1558', *Parliamentary History*, I (1982).

A. R. Myers, 'Parliament 1422–1509', in R. G. Davies and J. H. Denton (eds), *The English Parliament in the Later Middle Ages* (1981).

J. E. Neale, *Queen Elizabeth and her Parliaments*, (eds), 2 vols (1953–7).

W. Notestein, 'The winning of the initiative by the House of Commons', *Proceedings of the British Academy*, 11 (1926) – A thesis based on the development of the Committee of the Whole House. Not now generally accepted.

6 THE ROYAL COURT

S. Adams, 'Eliza enthroned', in C. Haigh (ed.), *The Reign of Elizabeth I* (1984).

S. Adams, 'Faction, clientage and party; English politics, 1550–1603', *History Today*, 32 (1982).

S. Anglo, *Spectacle, Pageantry and Early Tudor Policy* (1965) – An excellent chapter on Catherine of Aragon's entry in 1501.

D. Baker Smith, 'Inglorious glory; 1513 and the humanist attack on chivalry', in S. Anglo (ed.), *Chivalry in the Renaissance* (1990).

George Bull (ed.), *Castiglione's Book of the Courtier* (1967).

H. M. Colvin, *The History of the King's Works, IV, 1485–1660* (1982) – A comprehensive work of reference.

C. S. L. Davies, 'Provisions for armies, 1509–1550: a study in the effectiveness of early Tudor government', *Economic History Review*, 2nd series, 17 (1964–5).

John Dent, *The Quest for Nonsuch* (1962) – Report of the archaeological excavations in the 1950s.

M. Dowling, *Humanism in the Age of Henry VIII* (1986).

M. Dowling, 'The gospel and the court: reformation under Henry VIII', in P. Lake and M. Dowling (eds), *Protestantism and the National Church in Sixteenth-Century England* (1987).

Ian Dunlop, *Palaces and Progresses of Elizabeth I* (1962).

G. R. Elton, 'Points of contact: the court', in *Studies in Tudor and Stuart Politics and Government*, Vol. III (1983).

S. J. Gunn, *Charles Brandon, Duke of Suffolk, 1485–1545* (Oxford, 1988) – A good biography of Henry VIII's longest-surviving favourite.

S. J. Gunn and P. Lindley, *Cardinal Wolsey: Church, State and Art* (1991).

S. J. Gunn, 'Chivalry and the Politics of the Early Tudor Court', in *Chivalry in the Renaissance*, ed. S. Anglo (Woodbridge, 1990).

C. Haigh, *The Reign of Elizabeth I* (1984).

C. Haigh, *Elizabeth I* (1988).

D. E. Hoak, 'The secret history of the Tudor Court: the king's coffers and the king's purse, 1542–1553', *Journal of British Studies*, 26 (1987).

D. E. Hoak, 'The king's Privy Chamber, 1547–1553', in *Tudor Rule and Revolution*, ed. D. J. Guth and J. W. McKenna (Cambridge, 1982).

M. Howard, *The Early Tudor Country House: Architecture and Politics, 1490–1550* (1987).

M. E. James, 'English politics and the concept of honour, 1485–1642', *Past and Present*, supplement 3 (1978).

M. K. Jones and M. G. Underwood, *The King's Mother: Lady Margaret Beaufort, Countess of Richmond and Derby* (1992) – The only study of this extremely important woman.

G. Kipling, *The Triumph of Honour* (1977).

D. M. Loades, *The Tudor Court* (Bangor, 1991) – A structural study rather than a history.

R. C. McCoy, 'From the Tower to the tiltyard: Robert Dudley's return to glory', *Historical Journal*, 27 (1984).

A. R. Myers, *The Household Book of Edward IV* (1959) – Based upon the 'Black Book'. The only complete examination of the late medieval royal household.

J. Nichols, *The Progresses and Public Processions of Elizabeth* (1823) – Prints many documents.

J. G. Russell, *The Field of Cloth of Gold* (1969).

D. Starkey, *The Reign of Henry VIII: Politics and Personalities* (1985) – Lively and informative, but unreferenced.

D. Starkey, *The English Court from the Wars of the Roses to the Civil War* (1987) – A collection of essays, most of them valuable.

D. Starkey, (ed.), *Henry VIII: A European court in England* (1991).

R. Strong, *Splendour at Court* (1973).

A. Woodworth, *Purveyance for the Royal Household in the reign of Elizabeth* (Philadelphia, 1945).

7 THE SPECIAL JURISDICTIONS

B. Bradshaw, 'The Edwardian Reformation in Ireland', *Archivum Hibernicum*, 24 (1976–7).

B. Bradshaw, *The Irish Constitutional Revolution of the Sixteenth Century* (1979) – The fullest discussion of the changes of the 1530s and 1540s.

F. W. Brooks, 'The Cinque Ports', *Mariners Mirror*, 15 (1929).

F. W. Brooks, *The Council of the North* (1953) – A brief introduction.

M. L. Bush, 'The problem of the far north: a study in the crisis of 1537 and its consequences', *Northern History*, 6 (1971).

N. Canny, *The Elizabethan Conquest of Ireland: A Pattern Established, 1565–1576* (1976).

D. J. Clayton, 'The Administration of the County Palatine of Chester, 1442–1485', *Chetham Society*, 3rd series, 35 (1990).

C. G. Cruikshank, *Army Royal: An Account of Henry VIII's Invasion of France, 1513* (1969).

J. Davies, *Hanes Cymru* (1990) – The history of Wales, written in Welsh but now also available in English. The insider's view.

A. J. Eagleston, *The Channel Islands under Tudor Government* (Cambridge, 1949).

J. G. Edwards, *The Principality of Wales, 1267–1969* (Denbigh, 1969) – Strong on the medieval systems of government.

S. G. Ellis, 'Tudor policy and the Kildare ascendancy in the Lordship of Ireland, 1496–1534', *Irish Historical Studies*, 20 (1977).

S. G. Ellis, *Tudor Ireland* (1985) – The best textbook on the subject, but essentially an outsider's view. Summarises the findings of many years of research.

S. G. Ellis, *Reform and Revival: English Government in Ireland, 1470–1534* (1986).

S. G. Ellis, 'Crown, community and government in the English territories, 1450–1575', *History*, 71 (1986).

S. G. Ellis, 'A border baron: the rise and fall of Lord Dacre of the North', *Historical Journal*, 35 (1992).

S. G. Ellis, *Tudor Frontiers and Noble Power: The Making of the British State* (Oxford, 1995) – A comparison of the careers of Kildare and Dacre; argues that Henry VIII did not deal effectively with border regions.

G. R. Elton, 'Politics and the Pilgrimage of Grace', in *Studies in Tudor and Stuart Politics and Government*, Vol. III (1983) – Argues that it originated in court conspiracy.

C. Falls, *Elizabeth's Irish Wars* (1950).

R. A. Griffiths, *Rhys ap Thomas and his Family* (Cardiff, 1993) – The most powerful dynasty in South Wales in the early sixteenth century.

S. J. Gunn, 'The regime of Charles Brandon, Duke of Suffolk, in North Wales, and the reform of Welsh government, 1509–1525', *Welsh History Review*, 12 (1985).

R. W. Hoyle, 'Henry Percy, sixth Earl of Northumberland and the fall of the house of Percy', in *The Tudor Nobility*, ed. G. W. Bernard (Manchester, 1992).

L. Irwin, 'The Irish Presidency courts, 1569–1672', *The Irish Jurist*, new series, 12 (1977).

E. W. Ives, 'Court and county palatine in the reign of Henry VIII: the career of William Brereton of Malpas', *Transactions of the Historical Society of Lancashire and Cheshire*, 123 (1971).

M. E. James, *Change and Continuity in the Tudor North: The Rise of Thomas, First Lord Wharton* (York, 1965).

J. G. Jones, *Wales and the Tudor State* (Cardiff, 1988).

R. H. Kinvig, *A History of the Isle of Man* (Oxford, 1944) – Just about the only work on the subject.

D. E. Lowe, 'The Council of the Princes of Wales and the decline of the Herbert family during the second reign of Edward IV (1471–1483)', *Bulletin of the Board of Celtic Studies*, 27 (1977).

D. Marcombe (ed.), *The Last Palatinate* (Leicester, 1987).

R. G. Marsden, 'The Vice Admirals of the coasts', *English Historical Review*, 22 (1907).

K. M. E. Murray, *The Constitutional History of the Cinque Ports* (Manchester, 1935).

R. Reid, 'The rebellion of the northern Earls, 1569', *Transactions of the Royal Historical Society*, new series, 20 (1906).

W. R. B. Robinson, 'Early Tudor policy towards Wales: the acquisition of land and offices in Wales by Charles Somerset, Earl of Worcester', *Bulletin of the Board of Celtic Studies*, 20 (1962–3) and 21 (1964–6).

J. J. Silke, *Kinsale* (Liverpool, 1970) – Spanish involvement in the Tyrone rebellion, and the invasion of 1601.

R. Somerville, 'The Duchy of Lancaster Council and the Court of Duchy Chamber', *Transactions of the Royal Historical Society*, 4th series, 23 (1941).

R. Somerville, 'The palatinate courts in Lancashire', in A. Harding (ed.), *Law Making and Law Makers in British History* (1980).

M. Weiss, 'A power in the north? The Percies in the fifteenth century', *Historical Journal*, 19 (1976).

G. Williams, *Recovery, Reorientation and Reformation: Wales 1415–1642* (1987).

G. Williams, *Wales and the Acts of Union* (Bangor, 1992).

P. Williams, *The Council in the Marches of Wales under Elizabeth* (1958) – The best and most complete study of the Council in the Marches; also covers the earlier period.

8   REGIONAL AND PROVINCIAL IDENTITY

W. A. Bebb, *Cyfnod y Tuduraid* [*The Age of the Tudors*] (1939).

J. Beck, *Tudor Cheshire* (1968).

B. L. Beer, *Rebellion and Riot: Popular Disorders in England in the Reign of Edward VI* (1982).

J. Bossy, 'The Counter Reformation and the people of Catholic Ireland, 1596–1641', *Historical Studies*, 8 (1971).

B. Bradshaw, 'Native reaction to the Westward enterprise: a case study in Gaelic ideology', in K. R. Andrews, N. Canny and P. E. H. Hair (eds), *The Westward Enterprise* (1978).

M. St Clare Byrne, *Elizabethan Life in Town and Country* (1961).

N. P. Canny, *The Formation of the Old English Elite in Ireland* (1975).

P. Clark, *English Provincial Society from the Reformation to the Revolution* (1977) – The county of Kent.

T. J. Dunne, 'The Gaelic response to conquest and colonisation; the evidence of the poetry', *Studia Hibernica*, 20 (1980).

C. Haigh, *Reformation and Resistance in Tudor Lancashire* (1975) – The basic study of a 'different' English county. Argues that the reformation made almost no impact until the middle years of Elizabeth.

G. A. Hayes-McCoy, 'Gaelic society in Ireland in the late sixteenth century', *Historical Studies*, 4 (1963).

G. A. J. Hodgett, *Tudor Lincolnshire* (1975).

M. E. James, 'The murder at Cocklodge, 28th April 1489', *Durham University Journal*, 57 (1964–5) – The death of the 4th Earl of Northumberland and its political consequences.

G. H. Jenkins, *Hanes Cymru yn y Cyfnod Modern Cynnar, 1536–1760* [*The History of Wales in the Early Modern Period, 1536–1760*] (1983).

J. N. King, *English Reformation Literature* (Princeton, 1982) – The most satisfactory and accessible guide to the subject.

D. Matthew, *The Celtic Peoples of Renaissance Europe* (1933).

F. Rose-Troup, *The Western Rebellion of 1549* (1913) – Valuable appendix of documents.

D. B. Quinn, *The Elizabethans and the Irish* (1966).

W. S. K. Thomas, *Tudor Wales* (Cardiff, 1983).

R. Whiting, *The Blind Devotion of the People* (1989) – The diocese of Exeter. Argues that in the main the English people simply did what they were told during the Reformation.

G. Williams, *Welsh Reformation Essays* (Cardiff, 1967).

W. O. Williams, 'The survival of the Welsh language after the Union of England and Wales; the first phase, 1536–1642', *Welsh History Review*, 2 (1964).

Index

179